TRUST INC.

Robert T. Sicora

612-251-7766

robtsicora@gmail.com

TRUST INC.,

52 Weeks of Activities and Inspirations for Building Workplace Trust

Editor: **Barbara Brooks Kimmel**

Publisher: **Next Decade, Inc.**

ISBN: 978-1-932919-40-0
e-ISBN:978-1-932919-41-7

Next Decade books are available at special quantity discounts to use as premium and sales promotions or for use in corporate training programs. To contact a representative, please e-mail us at *Barbara@nextdecade.com*

Cover and interior design by Darlene Swanson, *www.van-garde.com*

Contents

Preface

I never expected to be editing our third book on organizational trust within a year of the release of our first *Trust Inc.: Strategies for Building Your Company's Most Valuable Asset*, published at the end of 2013, but there is an unlimited amount to learn and share on this topic. Our multiple award-winning flagship book brought over 30 experts together to explore the intersection of trust and leadership, trust and teams, and a host of other topics of interest to businesses, but applicable to all organizations.

This book was followed by our second in the spring of 2014. *Trust Inc., A Guide for Boards and C-Suites* is the collaborative work of dozens of experts who provide 100 practical tips on instilling trust "at the top." Many would argue that without "buy-in" from the Board and C-Suite, trust gets lost in the corporate culture.

And now I have the honor and privilege of contributing to and editing *Trust Inc., 52 Weeks of Activities and Inspirations for Building Workplace Trust*. As we enter the holiday season, this book, convening more than two dozen subject experts, is meant to be read and shared as a gift with those who choose to make trust a business imperative within their organization. Very simply, it provides an activity or inspiration to carry the reader through a full year.

I am passionate about trust and trustworthy organizations, and through Trust Across America we bring tools and programming to those who share our passion.

With the founding of Trust Across America – Trust Around the World in 2009 we began to tackle the challenges of organizational trust across cultural and generational boundaries, for-profit and not-for-profit organizations, government institutions, academia and the media. It's going to take a substantial collaborative effort to bring trust back to the heart of how we live and work. We believe this book is another important step towards that vision.

Would you like to help us?

Barbara Kimmel, Executive Director
Trust Across America – Trust Around the World

Acknowledgements

I would like to thank the contributors to this book who gave freely of their time and expertise. They are listed alphabetically.

Randy Conley

Peter C. DeMarco

Robert Galford

Charles H. Green

Ellen M. Hunt

Karin Hurt

Noreen J. Kelly

Barbara Brooks Kimmel

Jim Kouzes & Barry Posner

Holly Latty-Mann

Edward Marshall

Susan Mazza

Jon Mertz

Deborah Mills-Scofield

Dominique O'Rourke

Rosemary Perlmeter

Michael Randel

Drs. Dennis & Michelle Reina

Carol Sanford

Taina Savolainen

Laura Sicola

Brian Sooy

Jesse Stoner

Davia Temin

Robert Vanourek

Curtis C. Verschoor

Bob Whipple

Chapter 1
Leadership Activities & Inspirations

Listening for Leaders

Objective: Concretely demonstrate to leaders a way of interacting with others that increases influence through empathetic listening.

Requirements: 3 persons, each with a particular "difficult client/colleague" situation.

30 - 40 minutes elapsed time.

Can be done in multiples of three persons, with a strong facilitator.

Process overview: The exercise is done in three iterations. Each of the three gets a chance to role-play:

>Person A. a difficult client of their own

>Person B. an advisor or follower of the difficult client/colleague

>Person C. an observer

Each iteration proceeds as:

a.   60 seconds for the "client/colleague" person to describe the situation - out of role character

b.   4 minutes for the role-play – in character

c.   3 minutes debrief, led by the observer

Advance Instructions to Participants

- This is an exercise in listening for leadership and influence. The point of listening in this way is not to gain data or information and thus solve problems, but rather to understand fully the perspective of the client/colleague person.

- Each of you will get a chance to play your leader/listener role with someone else's real-life character; a chance to role-play one of your own real-life client or colleague; and a chance to observe two others act out a leader/follower interaction.

- The exercise will be done three times – each time, you'll play a different one of the three roles.

- When you are the client: be that person. Use their voice, their gestures. Empathize with them.

- When you are the leader/listener, your job is to listen for the full four minutes – and NOT to solve the problem. Do NOT drive for solutions.

- Observer: focus first on what the listener is doing well, then on giving constructive observations about what you saw happening.

Notes for Facilitators

In setting up the exercise:

- Note that the "advisor" character (Player B) is in effect playing the real world person of Player A (player A, recall, is playing their own client).

- Encourage the 60-second setup period to focus just on big picture description of the situation; don't get lost in technical detail

- Encourage the Player A to empathize with their client – mimic their body language and vocal styles.

- Tell the Player B that their fundamental job is to avoid solving the problem – just listen.

- Assume the meeting is set up in advance and goes straight to discussing the issue at hand.

Debrief Instructions to Participants

- First, the person who played the client/colleague – tell the other two people what it felt like to be listened to in this way, good or bad. Note: state how you *felt*, not what you *thought*.

- Second, the person who played the leader/listener: tell the other two what you found most difficult in listening for four minutes.

- Third, the observer: tell the listener what (s)he was doing well. How much time was spent listening / talking by each party? And did the discussion veer into problem-solving?

Wrap up by Facilitator

Ask the group what they felt was hardest about playing the listener role: almost certainly it will be "trying not to solve the problem." Underscore that a desire for problem-solving gets in the of way of the client/colleague feeling heard and understood. We need to suppress our desire to fix problems until the other party feels we have earned the right to offer advice.

Ask the group whether any of them felt a change in perspective by virtue of having had to role-play someone who gives them difficulty in relationships. This is a question of empathy: emphasize the importance of understanding others in being successful leaders. One can still disagree with others' actions and views, but to do so without comprehending their perspective will always reduce influence and harm leadership.

Charles H. Green

Charles H. Green is an author, speaker and world expert on trust-based relationships and sales in complex businesses. Founder and CEO of Trusted Advisor Associates, he is co-author of the classic *The Trusted Advisor* and its practical follow-up, *The Trusted Advisor Fieldbook*, and author of *Trust-based Selling*.

Leaders Must Listen

Trust is built in incremental steps. It begins with self-trust and flourishes when the leader listens to input from his team, creating shared values and goals that are accepted and adopted by all stakeholders.

Leaders must regularly communicate with stakeholders about the steps being taken to build trustworthy behavior within the organization.

Leaders must not confuse trust with compliance.

Most important, when building trust, leaders must be willing to listen to feedback and adjust their strategies accordingly.

Barbara Brooks Kimmel

Barbara Brooks Kimmel is the Executive Director of Trust Across America-Trust Around the World whose mission is to help organizations build trust. She is also the editor of the award winning TRUST INC. book series and the Executive Editor of TRUST! Magazine. In 2012 Barbara was named "One of 25 Women Changing the World" by Good Business International.

"Blue Ocean" Trust-Building Workshop (This Takes Guts)

Building trust requires courage: the courage to be vulnerable, to listen to feedback on what you, as a leader, do daily, and the resolve to follow through on your commitments to change, even if those changes are uncomfortable.

This trust-building activity takes guts because it opens you to feedback you may not have heard before. It's uncomfortable. This workshop, which I have used successfully, is a much shorter version of the excellent process described in the *Harvard Business Review* article "Blue Ocean Leadership" by W. Chan Kim and Renee Mauborgne.

This activity can be used in (1) large organizations that have several layers of management and several departments (or functional "silos"), or (2) individual departments. The workshop below, which may last a couple of hours, assumes the former as an example.

The senior leader in this workshop engages an objective facilitator for a session involving dozens of leaders at all levels in the leader's organization. Here are the steps involved:

"Blue Ocean" Trust-Building Workshop

1) The senior leader at the meeting announces that the purpose of the meeting is to positively influence the behaviors of all the leaders in the organization, including his or hers.

   a) Honest, constructive feedback is needed from everyone on what the top, middle, and front-line leaders are doing day-to-day.

   b) There will be no negative repercussions for the insights shared. That's a promise.

2) Four stations of the room are designated, perhaps the four corners of the room, and three flip charts on easels, or with pages posted on the wall, are at each corner.

   a) Each station has the flip chart pages titled:

      i.   Top management on one page

      ii. Middle management on another page

      iii. Front-line management on the final page

b)   Under the management title are four quadrants spaced out with the subtitles: Stop, Less, More, and Begin

    i.   A sample page may look like this:

Top Mgt.	
Stop	More
Less	Begin

1)   The facilitator divides the group of participants into four smaller groups each consisting of representatives of their management rank. So, two groups of front-line managers may be at two locations respectively, while a single group of middle managers are at another, and a single group of top managers may be at the fourth station.

a)   The most senior leader should excuse them self from the room for this portion of the exercise.

2)   Each group spends five to ten minutes at their first station, writing on the flip chart page what they think the manager level indicated on the chart should:

a)   Stop doing (e.g., micro-managing)

b)   Do less of (e.g., spending time in meetings)

c)   Do more of (e.g., praising trust-building activities of individuals)

d)   Begin doing (e.g., putting trust on the agenda for periodic discussion)

3)   After five to ten minutes, the facilitator rotates each group to spend five to ten minutes at the next station, adding their ideas, building on the ideas already marked there, until all four groups have visited all four stations.[2]

4)   Then the facilitator reassembles the entire group, including the senior

leader, to tour all the flip charts around the room, facilitating a discussion of what is there, circling, underlining, adding clarifications, and making any group-recommended alterations.

    a)   The senior leader(s) should ask clarifying questions but not engage in defensive remarks.

5)   From these notes and modifications, a summary list of "Next Steps" can be created by the group and documented by the facilitator of what each level of management will commit to stop doing, do less of, more of, and begin doing.

    a)   This is the critical "Commitment Stage" for each level of management, who should also agree to report back periodically to the group on progress they have made on their "commitments."

The benefit of this short workshop is that participants can, perhaps for the first time, and in a safe, group environment, express their feelings about what leaders at all organizational levels are actually doing, or should be doing.

The challenge with this workshop is that it may provide some uncomfortable (but essential) feedback to all levels of leadership.

Changing behavior, stopping or lessening negative behaviors, or doing more of, or beginning to do positive behaviors, is hard because many management habits are deeply ingrained. But once a group has spoken out about what they want more of and less of, and *once those results are actually delivered*, then trust is built, engagement is enhanced, and more heart-driven commitments are made by the people involved.

This shorter, Blue Ocean workshop is not a replacement for the deeper dive into Blue Ocean Leadership as well described by Chen and Mauborgne in their *HBR* article, but I have found it to be a highly effective way of building organizational trust.

Bob Vanourek

Bob Vanourek is the former CEO of five firms from a start-up to a billion dollar NY stock exchange turnaround. He is an organizational consultant and is one of Trust Across America's Top 100 Thought Leaders in Trustworthy Business Behavior. He is the co-author of the award-winning book *Triple Crown Leadership: Building Excellent, Ethical, and Enduring Organizations.* www.triplecrownleadership.com Contact info@triplecrownleadership for further assistance.

(Endnotes)
1. http://hbr.org/2014/05/blue-ocean-leadership/ar/1

2. This technique is known a "brainwalking," invented by innovation consultant and author Bryan Mattimore. Brainwalking is preferred to seated brainstorming because it gets people up and moving and has them divided into smaller groups where it is easier to express ideas. See *Idea Stormers* by Bryan Mattimore, pp. 25-29, for an explanation of brainwalking.

Trustworthiness in Action: Build it Using these 10 "Ts"

#1 Trustworthy leadership – Very simply, a culture of trust cannot exist with an untrustworthy leader.

#2 Transformation – Productivity and execution begin when the CEO creates a set of values and goals that are shared, accepted and adopted by all stakeholders.

#3 Tools – There are many trust tools CEOs can use to build trust with their internal and external stakeholders. These run the gamut from metrics and assessments to online surveys.

#4 Treatment – The Golden Rule says to "treat others the way you want to be treated." This certainly holds true for trust.

#5 Teamwork – Teamwork leads to better decisions and better outcomes. Teams create trust, and trust creates teams.

#6 Talk – Your stakeholders need to know what steps you are taking to build a trustworthy organization. Quarterly numbers are no longer the be all and end all.

#7 Truth – Truth-telling is at the core of trust. Any CEO who wants to build a trustworthy organization must have an extremely comfortable relationship with the truth.

#8 Time – Building a culture of trustworthy business does not happen overnight. It takes time, maybe even years – but not decades.

#9 Transparency – Merriam Webster defines "transparent" as visibility or accessibility of information, especially with business practices. Any CEO who thinks he or she can still hide behind a veil of secrecy need only spend a few minutes on social media reading what their stakeholders are saying.

#10 Thoughtful – Not all stakeholders need to know the company's trade secrets, or what the CEO had for dinner. But if your company is serious about increasing trustworthiness, consider engaging all your stakeholders in rich, thoughtful conversations.

Barbara Brooks Kimmel

Barbara Brooks Kimmel is the Executive Director of Trust Across America-Trust Around the World whose mission is to help organizations build trust. She is also the editor of the award winning TRUST INC. book series and the Executive Editor of TRUST! Magazine. In 2012 Barbara was named "One of 25 Women Changing the World" by Good Business International.

You Can't Take Trust for Granted

Every single relationship is built on trust. It's foundational. It's fundamental. And foundations and fundamentals need constant attention. Building trust is a process that begins when someone is willing to risk being the first to open up, being the first to show vulnerability, and being the first to let go of control—and then reciprocating these actions. And in the leader-constituent relationship, leaders go first. If you want the high levels of performance that come with trust and collaboration, you have to be the first to demonstrate your trust in others before asking them to trust you.

Jim Kouzes and Barry Posner

Jim Kouzes and Barry Posner are coauthors of the award-winning and best-selling book, *The Leadership Challenge*, and over thirty other books and workbooks on leadership. Jim is the Dean's Executive Fellow of Leadership and Barry is the Acolti Chaired Professor of Leadership, Leavey School of Business, Santa Clara University.

The Smallest Deed is Better than the Greatest Promise

"In daily leadership work, it is the small deeds and words that make a difference in leading by trust – not the great promises!"

Objective:

- Inspire and encourage leaders to grow in self-awareness of the crucial role of trust, and developing ways of enacting trust in daily leadership work.

- Provide real life study material for ideas and advice to leaders in building, sustaining and repairing trust.

Who can benefit: Applies to leadership situations in workplace relationships for those

- Who want to influence their followers and increase leader effectiveness by trust building and sustaining.

- Who want to learn more of mistrust and understand how trust is repaired.

- Who are in a particular situation with a "difficult subordinate/ colleague", etc.

Real life study material:

Material below is for leaders to learn, and pick up ideas for trust-building. A case and brief personal stories are told or written by leaders and followers in different workplaces consisting of experiences & feelings of trusting in everyday situations.

Case: Trust-building and communication

This case is about international project leadership focusing on the communication issues in trust-building. The project aimed to strengthen the infrastructure for quality in several countries. Case material and data is based on interviews, project documents, participant observation, memos and study diary.

The project team involves four main actors: the project team leader, contracting authority, consultancy firm managing the project, and donator. At the finishing stage of the project, change occurred in the project team organization when the leader resigned. A public process was open for hiring a new one. The main stakeholders requested the consultancy firm to assess potential internal candidates for a position. Five candidates were presented, one internal and four external.

Since the beginning of the recruiting process, the internal candidate felt that the consultancy firm had no interest in him. There was no meeting, no call, just an email requesting his CV and several later emails. Contractual conditions were pending with asymmetric negotiation situation. The consultancy firm did not communicate with the project team and emails were not answered. After three months, one of the directors visited the project team on site – at the time when the internal candidate was not in the country. Mistrust increased shown in the candidate's talk: *"It is harmful that he will come when I'll not be around, as he said one of his goals is to really know the team and how the project is performing. This way of acting looks unconvincing."*

The contracting authority involved in the process decided to appoint the internal candidate as a team leader. After that the consultancy firm communicated the decision to the candidate by email addressed to the whole team and without any preceding personal communication (email, phone, f-to-f). The only email from the consultancy firm requested the candidate to prepare an extra report even before he took up his new position. Finally, the situation developed into a total break in communication and lead to a trust breach between the consultancy firm and the then appointed team leader, and also towards the other main stakeholders. As a consequence, all stakeholders experienced deep uncertainty, and mistrust affected moral, productivity and project group cohesion.

Then the contracting authority took a role in the conflict resolving and *trust restoring* by forcing the main actors to find a solution. At this point the director from the consultancy firm contacted the team leader by phone which somewhat improved communication. Two months later another director visited the project. Through face-to-face communication some misunderstandings were clarified and foundations laid to restore trust in relationships. However, restoring trust with all actors involved may take time.

Brief stories:

Manager: Trust is a very important issue. Writing about my personal experiences of trust inspired me to thinking trust more and raise the issue in common workplace meetings. I also intend to start a discussion with my subordinates in the team and collect their experiences, desires and needs of trusting.

Manager: If you lose trust for some reason or another you cannot restore trust all alone. Trust should be earned and repair takes time. If or when trust is violated, it may need a long repair process before the situation gets balanced. It may be also the case that broken trust may not be restored to the level it used to be in leader-follower relationship meaning that trust is really worth sustaining.

Employee: I am going through a difficult situation, as I have trusted in my boss and now I feel betrayed. I shared confidential issues in e-mail to my boss that was not meant for anyone else. Too bad he forwarded e-mail, and the worst of all, to the large group. 'A lump in my throat' I felt so bad. I could not do anything else but tell my boss what happened and how I felt. My boss did not even realize he had done something wrong. I felt helpless and mistrusted and decided not to trust in him like before.

How to proceed and what to do:
Study material can be processed in several ways as follows:

A.   As *self-study* and learning reflecting one's own experiences and feelings, etc. and developing applications for daily leadership work.

B.   As interactive *group study with fellow leaders* by pre-reading material first and then getting together for reflections, talking and sharing ideas and applications & lessons learned.

C.   *With a follower* in two ways:

1.   Bring up a conversation on the trust issues, recommended especially if trust violation or breach has already occurred and a need for restoration exists. Initiating conversation is a leader responsibility.

2.   Talk with a follower to get experiences, and suggestions for improvement. Meeting can be prepared by encouraging the follower to write his/her own trust story beforehand in a selected workplace relationship. This may be helpful in challenging/special situations when talking is too risky or impossible. In face-to-face discussion experiences and feelings are shared for improving/resolving the issues that may come up.

D.   Most important is to listen and understand fully the views/experiences and feelings of the person/-s involved.

Final encouragement:

The smallest deed is better than the greatest promise. Start off small, one deed at a time. Utilize the power of small daily words and grow in time bringing the followers delight and your business improved competitiveness.

Taina Savolainen

Taina Savolainen, Professor of Management and Leadership, University of Eastern Finland, Business School; Leader of the research group "Trust within Organizations". Trust researcher and educator of inter-personal trust in leadership and workplace relationships.

http://uef.academia.edu/TainaSavolainen

www.linkedin.com/pub/taina-savolainen/1a/778/ba4

"BE" Trustworthy: 20 Steps

Trust is the essence of leadership
– Colin Powell

Let's face it, being a trustworthy leader and leading a trustworthy organization are not rocket science. The biggest problem with trust is that it is not "regulated" and therefore, most leaders don't think about it. Trust is taken for granted. Imagine if CEO compensation was tied to an annual trust audit!

The second biggest problem is an outcome of the first. When trust is not practiced proactively or when a leader hasn't "banked" trust, he or she spends a good deal of time putting out fires and reacting to crises. There is no time to build trust into the organizational DNA.

Regardless of the size or type of organization you lead, choosing trust as a business imperative means the strategy starts with you. Begin today by following these simple suggestions:

- Be honest: Once you tell a lie, nobody will believe anything you say.
- Be selfless: Put others before yourself – ask how you can help and mean it.
- Be humble: Park your ego at the door.
- Be inclusive: Celebrate and share the successes of others.
- Be accountable: Always keep your word.
- Be appreciative: Never forget the "Thank you."
- Be apologetic: Admit your mistakes.
- Be competent: It's okay to say "I don't know."
- Be consistent: Always lead the same way.
- Be patient: Take time to teach.
- Be persistent: Build trust into the daily agenda.
- Be open-minded: Sometimes change is good.
- Be positive: People like being around others who are.
- Be curious: Learn from others.

- Be risk tolerant: Innovation flourishes when people are allowed to make mistakes.

- Be transparent: Let others know what you are thinking.

- Be authentic: Don't be a phony.

- Be an enabler: Allow people to make independent decisions.

- Be human: Share personal stories with your team.

- Be fun: And finally, don't forget to laugh at your own mistakes and enjoy the journey with your team.

Barbara Brooks Kimmel

Barbara Brooks Kimmel is the Executive Director of Trust Across America-Trust Around the World whose mission is to help organizations build trust. She is also the editor of the award winning TRUST INC. book series and the Executive Editor of TRUST! Magazine. In 2012 Barbara was named "One of 25 Women Changing the World" by Good Business International.

The Cycle of Trust

Relational trust and organizational trust are dependent on four key stages we call the *cycle of trust*. *Relational trust* refers to the ways individuals form relationships necessary for the organization to function as a whole in pursuit of its intended purpose. *Organizational trust* refers to the ways that individuals outside the organization (customers, shareholders and other stakeholders) come to trust the organization without knowing if it possesses all of the essential parts needed to fulfill its purpose.

A cycle is a series of events that are often repeated in the same order. Trust, as a natural cycle, includes four key events:

- **Extending trust:** The trustor (the person extending trust) chooses to extend trust. It is the actualization of the trustor's attitude and judgment through choice (or surrender) toward another person or thing.

- **Building trust:** Inspiring, gaining and influencing others' attitudes and judgments of trust through communication (verbal, written, behavioral, etc.)

- **Sustaining trust:** Reinforcing trust on the deepest level through adherence to the recognized principles and the ethics of the organization.

- **Restoring trust:** The process of restoring not the trust itself, but the communications that support trust.

The cycle of trust is like any physical workout: It must be eased into carefully to avoid flexing the muscles beyond their ability. In other words, each person first *extends trust* only to the extent that he or she is freely able to do so. As both trustor and trustee successfully complete each step of the cycle, their trust relationship can be flexed to accommodate greater capacities.

Of course, we must continue to extend trust to develop the trust relationship, but we can also withdraw or begin to qualify the trust we have extended. The second step of the trust cycle, *building trust,* occurs through continued communications that inspire, gain and influence others' attitudes and judgments of trust. As we practice these first two steps, we layer on the third, *sustaining trust.* This step includes a notable addition: The trustor must demonstrate that he or she operates from recognized organizational principles and ethics. While this cycle of trust serves to establish healthy trust relationships, it is never truly complete because it grows through repeating the four stages of extending, building, sustaining and—since no one is perfect—restoring trust when necessary.

Leaders, in particular, must seek meaningful ways to extend, build and sustain trust with others. A practical way to think about trust is to distinguish between how we tend to trust ourselves versus how we tend to trust others. Most people form *intentions* based on trust in their self-perceived ability to follow through and achieve the intended aim. If a leader misjudges his own decision-making abilities, even his *self*-trust can be damaged (and rightly so) until he reflects and re-examines the mistake. And, since our *actions* are the best indication of our nature, followers also distrust a leader who fails to achieve his or her intended results.

	Extending	Building	Sustaining	Restoring
Trusting Ourselves	INTENTIONS	ACTIONS	RESULTS	HABITS of EXCELLENCE
Trusting Others	ACTIONS	RESULTS	INTENTIONS	RESTITUTION

Once we understand that others extend trust to us based on our *actions*, then we realize the importance of delivering the necessary results. When these results are good, trust relationships deepen and trust is sustained because the leader's *intent* aligns with his or her *actions*. This understanding is critical for allowing us to extend trust in situations where explicit direction or verifiable results aren't always available. Of course, no leader is perfect; we all make mistakes or willfully harm others, breaking or damaging trust as a result. In these cases, leaders must both *apologize* for the damage done and work to *restore* the trust, using the trust cycle to flex and build the trust relationship.

The best teams build trust because they act on the leader's *intent*—empathy is a strong dynamic at work. Followers know what the leader needs, and align their actions accordingly. Reciprocally, the leader understands followers' intentions, and sustains their trust by ensuring his or her actions and results are aligned with meeting followers' needs.

Peter C. DeMarco

Peter C. DeMarco is the founder of Priority Thinking® (pdemarco@ prioritythinking.com), a provider of leadership coaching, organizational development, strategy and ethics education programs to businesses, organizations and MBA programs. He also teaches leadership and ethics at the Fuqua School of Business at Duke University and St. John Fisher College.

Ten Questions For Leaders Seeking to Build Trustworthy Organizations

1. Am I trustworthy? Does trust matter to me as an individual or in my professional life?

2. Is trust mentioned in our mission statement or corporate credo?

3. Do all stakeholders view me as trustworthy? Have I asked?

4. Do I talk about the importance of trust on a regular basis?

5. Do I engage my employees in discussions about trust?

6. Am I transparent?

7. Do I celebrate achievements? Do I allow mistakes?

8. Am I more concerned with profits or values?

9. Would I compromise my integrity?

10. Do I acknowledge the business case for trust?

Barbara Brooks Kimmel

Barbara Brooks Kimmel is the Executive Director of Trust Across America-Trust Around the World whose mission is to help organizations build trust. She is also the editor of the award winning TRUST INC. book series and the Executive Editor of TRUST! Magazine. In 2012 Barbara was named "One of 25 Women Changing the World" by Good Business International.

What's Your Strategic Trust Alignment (STA) Quotient?

This trust diagnostic tool is designed to help you understand where you are as a leader on the Trust Continuum.

The following trust elements and imperatives reflect the author's Trust in Business Model:

- *Three Elements of Trust:* Relationships, Communication and Sharing & Collaboration

- *Seven Imperatives of Trust:* Accountability, Authenticity, Credibility, Honesty, Integrity, Respect and Transparency

For each category below, rate yourself on these trust elements and trust imperatives, based on your workplace interactions and specific role (CEO, manager, supervisor, team/group member or employee/associate/individual contributor).

For each question, rate your answer on a scale of 1 to 5:
1 = Not at all
5 = To a very great extent
Place your score in the fields provided.

Trust Elements

Relationships

- Values people's input and opinions _____

- Treats everyone with equal consideration, regardless of their level in the organization _____

- Helps to ease conflict and tension in the workplace _____

  Sub Total _____

Communication

- Engages in clear, effective communication / shares the context around the message to provide explanation and background _____

- Creates open dialogue to ensure understanding / encourages opportunity for candid feedback

- Practices consistency and alignment of written and verbal messages

_____

Sub Total _____

Sharing & Collaboration

- Shares information and resources frequently and openly _____
- Involves others in the ownership of ideas and planning process

_____

- Promotes collaboration _____

Sub Total _____

Trust Imperatives

Accountability

- Accountable for my actions, words, decisions and promised project dates/timelines _____
- Admits mistakes and acknowledge project missteps _____
- Holds myself accountable to the same standards I establish for others

_____

Sub Total _____

Authenticity

- Engages in honest conversations _____
- Demonstrates company's values through my thoughts, words, intentions and actions _____
- Brings words and actions into alignment (do what I say I will do)

_____

Sub Total _____

Credibility

- Am trustworthy _____
- Walks the talk _____
- Inspires confidence through my actions and behavior _____

Sub Total _____

Honesty

- Tells the truth _____
- Communicates simply, straightforwardly and consistently across the entire audience _____
- I say what I know, when I know it. If I don't know, I say so. If I can't tell, I say so _____

  Sub Total _____

Integrity

- Follows through on commitments and promises _____
- Practices and promotes alignment with the organization's values

  _____
- Takes responsibility for my actions and acts ethically _____

  Sub Total _____

Respect

- Promotes mutual trust and cooperation _____
- Inclusive _____
- Acknowledges and honor people's feelings and concerns _____

  Sub Total _____

Transparency

- Open _____
- Visible _____
- Discloses information as needed _____

  Sub Total _____

Your Strategic Trust Quotient (STA):
Grand Total (out of a total possible 150) _____

Based on your results, you can identify where you are strong in trust building practices. This is a starting point for creating an action plan to develop trusting relationships that yield the highest performance.

The first step in any trusting relationship is to know and understand. Greater understanding of where you are on the trust continuum at work will lead to improved relationships with colleagues, more positive connections with staff and increased trust with customers.

Put Yourself and your Team on the Trust Track!

Here's a set of quick Self-Assessment questions to ask Individuals/Organizational Leaders:

Questions to ask individuals. Am I ...

Thoughtful? **T**rustworthy?

Responsible? **R**eliable?

Understanding? **U**sing my skills and knowledge to help/collaborate with others?

Selfless? **S**haring information?

Truthful? **T**aking responsibility for my words and actions?

Questions to ask organizational leaders. Am I ...

Thorough? **T**ransparent?

Responsive? **R**espectful?

Unyielding? **U**tilizing input from my employees/associates?

Systematic? **S**etting the same standards for myself that I establish for others?

Timely? **T**elling the truth?

Noreen J. Kelly

Noreen J. Kelly, President of Noreen Kelly Coaching & Consulting, helps leaders build trust through communication. She has promoted new initiatives for organizations of all sizes, led change communication efforts to major organizations and provided communications counsel to senior executives and mid-level leaders on employee engagement issues. For more information, see: www.noreenkelly.com Noreen can be reached at: noreen@noreenkelly.com

What Role Does Trust Play in Your Organization?

Answer the following questions and share the answers with your team. Ask for feedback. Analyze the responses where your answers are not fully aligned with your team members. Work together to create a long-term plan to make trust a business imperative.

SUCCESS: What role does trust play in ensuring the success of your organization?

PERFORMANCE: How is trust tied to high performance, innovation, and sustainability in your organization?

COSTS: What are the costs/implications of not having a high level of trust in your organization?

BENEFITS: What are the payoffs of a trust-based organization for the workforce, customers, leadership and shareholders?

COLLABORATION: How do you transform a siloed, reactive, heroic leadership culture to one that is trust-based, team-focused, and collaborative?

CULTURE: What values, principles or beliefs does your organization follow that are essential to building a foundation of trust?

ACTION: What are the key actions that characterize your commitment to building stakeholder trust?

LEADERSHIP: Which do you consider your "Best Practice" in trustworthy business behavior – the strategy that separates you from your competitors?

TRANSFORMATION: What types of leadership behaviors build high trust and collaboration in your organization?

PROOF: What verifiable evidence can you provide that these trust actions create substantive and positive impacts for stakeholders?

VISION: How will your trust building practices grow over the next five years?

Barbara Brooks Kimmel

Barbara Brooks Kimmel is the Executive Director of Trust Across America-Trust Around the World whose mission is to help organizations build trust. She is also the editor of the award winning TRUST INC. book series and the Executive Editor of TRUST! Magazine. In 2012 Barbara was named "One of 25 Women Changing the World" by Good Business International.

Validating the Values of Others Most Different

The best activity we have used to encourage new urban school leaders to build trust with their veteran teachers is to ask them to describe a large challenge they are facing that requires change. We then ask them to identify those who are likely to be opposed to the change they plan to make in order to overcome the challenge. Once the young leader identifies the likely opposers we ask them to identify what these opposers may value that causes them to resist the change that is requested of them.

Often public leaders are blind to the values of their resisters and must rewrite their narrative several times before accomplishing their task.

Once they do this the hard work begins. We ask them to identify what they have to change about themselves, given these competing values, to gain the trust of their resisters. This may consist of listening to a story they don't want to hear or reconciling a wrong that has been overlooked in the hurried pace of the work.

This is the most powerful activity we have found for motivating urban leaders to listen with receptivity and patience and to increasing transparency between those in a position of authority and those that have limited positional authority.

Rosemary Perlmeter

Rosemary Perlmeter, Co-Founder & CEO, of the Teaching Trust, has spent the last seventeen years working on public education initiatives in Texas. This work began in 1996 when she joined with the former mayor of Irving and community leaders to open and operate a dynamic non-profit known today as Uplift Education, one of the first and most successful charter school operators in Texas.

Don't Take Trust for Granted

Do these headlines look familiar? They were pulled from the news in a period of under 24 hours.

Football Must Regain the Public's Trust

Trust Vital Between Officers & The Community

State Audit of Fayette Schools Shows Need to Restore Public Trust

Restore Public Trust

The headlines rarely change. Everyday we hear about the need to restore trust in education, communities, sports, business and government. The story is the same, only the names of the violators change. I can't think of a single headline that ever read something like this " We are Embracing Trust as a Business Imperative and Building it Into Our Foundation."

There is enormous societal confusion swirling around the term "trust" that stems from this "restoration" approach. It is based on the assumption that trust was present before the crisis. In almost every case it wasn't. Building a foundation of trust is a proactive decision made by the leaders of an organization, and it is built in incremental steps. In every one of the headlines above, I will venture to guess that trust was never a component of the leadership agenda, nor its Board of Directors.

Unfortunately, trust is taken for granted. It is assumed that it just "exists" when, in reality, it rarely does. Some leaders might argue, "Why bother? Maybe we'll get lucky and never face a crisis." I would respond that it's much less expensive to build a foundation of trust, than it is to "manage" a crisis and attempt to build trust after the crisis. Building a foundation of trust also brings tangible and intangible benefits. These are just a few:

- Improved collaboration driving decision-making speed, efficiency and innovation
- Greater personal effectiveness for all involved, improving team projects and the odds of their coming to fruition
- Increased employee responsibility and competence
- Improved morale
- Faster/more efficient new business development
- Win/win opportunities both internally and externally

These are some pretty good reasons for building a foundation of trust. Don't you agree? And remember, you CANNOT regain or restore something that never existed.

Barbara Brooks Kimmel

Barbara Brooks Kimmel is the Executive Director of Trust Across America-Trust Around the World whose mission is to help organizations build trust. She is also the editor of the award winning TRUST INC. book series and the Executive Editor of TRUST! Magazine. In 2012 Barbara was named "One of 25 Women Changing the World" by Good Business International.

Experiment-Learn-Apply-Iterate

Taking risk requires many levels of trust. First, a series of "right" choices: right questions, right methods for discovering answers, right people, right processes, etc. Second, trust in uncertainty and imperfection: being ok with maybe never having the 'right' answer or 'perfect' solution. That's why learning how to inexpensively and quickly Experiment-Learn-Apply-Iterate is critical to building trust muscles.

Experiment: Identify a market, customer segment and/or business model that needs shaking up. Don't start by focusing on the solution, the product or service, but on the needs of the customer/market. I call this *"Rushing to Discover, Not to Solve."* Create a cross-functional team with air cover so they are free to try things.

1. Focus on learning as much as possible about what the customers need to have done, called "Jobs-To-Be-Done" (JTBD), the pains they have because they don't have a [great] solution and the gains they can have with a great solution. Don't focus on the product or service yet!!! Focus on the customers' real problems, the obstacles, context and constraints to accomplishing that job. Get out of the office and into the real world! Observe – watch *what* customers do/don't do, *how* they do/don't do 'it', what is going on around them *when* they are trying to do/not do it. Don't give advice or tell them what to do. Just observe, ask questions to clarify, understand and get a sense of each JTBD's importance and level of dissatisfaction with the current state.

2. Take your observations and, using Value Proposition Design (a companion to Business Model Generation), fill in the JTBD, the pains and gains for each customer segment. Based on prioritizing the importance of these, brainstorm possible solutions that will address the most important and most dissatisfying JTBD. Don't worry right now about how easy it is to do create these solutions; that's for later. At this point, your prioritizations and possible solutions are all hypotheses!

3. Create prototypes of the possible solutions to test with customers, such as tangible objects you can mock up (e.g., cardboard and duct tape, 3D printing, etc.), animations of the possible solution in use, screenshots, simplified websites or applications, etc. Remember, this is a prototype, not the final product or solution. The purpose is to test your hypotheses on the critical JTBD, pains and gains through the prototype. Do not let perfection be the enemy of

accomplishment! The prototype doesn't need to include everything, just the features critical to testing the hypotheses. Now take your prototypes out into the world and test them with customers!

Learn: Watch how your customers respond to your prototype. Remember, this is still an experiment and you're still testing hypotheses. Also remember that until a customer actually gives you money, any "willingness to pay" has a huge margin of error. Watch them use it, touch it, interact with it. Watch how they respond to what it does/doesn't do, where their eyes go first, where they seem stumped or frustrated, where they seem excited. Ask questions to clarify and understand, not to advise or judge.

Apply: Take the learning above and apply them to your Value Proposition Design Canvas. You will be wrong about a lot of things! The VP Canvas will definitely change. Redo the prototype based on those learnings, go back to your customers and test it again. Remember – the purpose is to test your hypotheses so you can create a solution that really meets your customers needs, not your needs.

Iterate: Repeat Experiment-Learn-Apply until you are able to create a meaningful, valuable solution for your customers or determine you can't. As you get more confident on your solution, start building out the rest of the Business Model using the Business Model Canvas.

The ELAI model is pretty straightforward. Don't overcomplicate it. Get out and do it! You'll be surprised at the level of trust and know-how you create!

Deborah Mills-Scofield

Deborah Mills-Scofield has her own consultancy on innovation and strategy & is a partner in a Venture Capital firm. Deb writes for Harvard Business Review, Switch and Shift & other venues, including her blog, & has contributed to several books. She is on the board of BIF, RISD's DESINE-Lab & Brown University's Engineering School, lectures in Brown's IE-Brown E-MBA program, mentors STEAM students & those doing 'regular' & social startups. Her Bell Labs patent was one of AT&T & Lucent's highest-revenue generating patents. She can be reached at @dscofield or dms@mills-scofield.com.

Trustworthy Culture & Leadership Character

Successful leadership is not about being tough or soft, sensitive or assertive, but about a set of attributes. First and foremost is character.
— Warren Bennis

Ask any group of people whom they trust and the two most common answers will be "parents" and "siblings." Ask them why and they will talk about longevity, familiarity and shared experiences. Rarely will the answer to the first question be a coworker or a boss.

What makes families unique? Each has its own culture. But if the family culture is corrupt, so are the offspring. The same applies to organizations, regardless of their size, industry or composition.

Someone recently asked me if there were any "quick fixes" for low-trust organizations. My answer was simply "Diseases can't be cured with Band Aids." Trust takes time and it is built in incremental steps.

If you lead an organization and want to build trust into its DNA, it all begins (and ends) with you.

Start with an assessment of yourself:

- Are you trustworthy?
- Do you have integrity, character and values?
- Do you share those values with your family?
- Do you instill them in your children?
- Do you take your personal values to work?

Perform an organizational trust audit:

- Have you built trust into your organizational culture with the support of your Board?
- Is it reflected in your statement of values and credo?
- How do you practice it?
- How well do you communicate it?
- Can it outlive you?

Consider your internal stakeholders:

- Do you discuss trust daily?
- Do you encourage feedback?
- Do you share a consistent vision?
- Do you model openness and vulnerability?
- Do you use transparent decision-making?
- Do you ask for input?
- Do you have long-term trust-building goals and execute them well, one by one?
- Do you share every "Wow" moment in your organization?
- Do you communicate, communicate, communicate?

Consider your external stakeholders:

- Have you shared your vision and values in building a trustworthy organization?
- Have you identified the outcome(s) you are seeking?
- Have you defined your intentions for each of our stakeholder groups?
- Have you made promises that you will keep?
- Have you determined the steps you will take to fulfill these promises?

Remember, the fish rots from the head. Every problem in an organization, including low trust, can be traced back to its leadership.

Barbara Brooks Kimmel

Barbara Brooks Kimmel is the Executive Director of Trust Across America-Trust Around the World whose mission is to help organizations build trust. She is also the editor of the award winning TRUST INC. book series and the Executive Editor of TRUST! Magazine. In 2012 Barbara was named "One of 25 Women Changing the World" by Good Business International.

Chapter 2

Teamwork Activities & Inspirations

Uncovering Shared Motivation Builds Common Ground in Teams

People can sometimes question whether other members of the team are as committed as themselves to the team's work. The process of discovering they have Shared Values can be a great boost to the experience of Trust in the team. Here's a simple activity to help a team uncover the Values they have in common.

- Identify the context of the team's work.

- Begin by reminding people of the team's purpose and the mission of the organization. This is the context for their work together. In some teams, this may be a familiar context. In other teams, it can help focus them around the reasons the team has been established.

- Invite each team member to tell a story that describes the values that led to them doing this work.

- The invitation to tell a story allows people to tap into their motivating values, the yearning that led them (and keeps them) in a particular field of work. Starting with a story also makes it easier for people to tease out their values as they are not always explicit, even to themselves.

- Support team members in identifying the common values in the stories they have heard.

- Allow team members time to discuss the pattern, or the themes, in the stories they have heard. Help them to sort through these themes and to inquire of one another for more information in ways that help the values become more visible.

- Name and Celebrate these Shared Values.

- Once the common values in the team have been identified and named, they can be productively used to build further bridges between members of the team. While it may be necessary to acknowledge that these are not the only values held by people in the team, they serve as an important foundation, as common ground, in the work the team will be doing together.

Let's illustrate the benefits of this activity with a story. My company was asked to work with a team responsible for conducting clinical trials in a global pharmaceutical company. Team members were dispersed to different locations around the world and they were experiencing a significant level of conflict. Trust was a casualty as communication broke down and relationships eroded.

We designed a face-to-face meeting to which all members of the team were invited and we decided to use this Values-Sharing activity as the opening exercise of the meeting. We believed that if the team members could become aware of their common values, they would have a greater appreciation for one another and an increased ability to listen to each other more respectfully.

Each member of the team took a turn to introduce themselves and their story. Some spoke in a matter of fact way about how their professional journey had unfolded to result in their current work. Others spoke with great emotion of early experiences seeing a parent or another family member struggle with their health, and how this had motivated them to enter the healthcare field.

Team members listened carefully to one another, and they noticed the different reasons for their interest in the healthcare field. They were soon able to name an emerging pattern, that many of them were drawn into this field of work because they wanted to reduce and relieve suffering among people. This shared insight was a breakthrough in their interactions with one another. They had previously been suspicious of one another's motives, but now they were faced with the realization that they were all motivated by the same thing – to ensure the safe development of new vaccines and treatments that would reduce sickness and suffering. With this common foundation, they were able to face the hard work of re-building trust with one another and becoming a world-class team in which they all did their work with pride.

Michael Randel

Michael Randel is an organization development consultant who leads organizations through change and growth. He was recognized as a "Top 100 Thought Leader in Trustworthy Business" in 2014. Based in Washington DC, he works locally and globally. You can reach him at Michael@RandelConsultingAssociates.com.

If You Want to Build Trust, Don't Just Show Up

In business, it's easy to just show up.

- Show up at a lunch
- Show up at a conference
- Show up at a meeting
- Show up at a webinar
- Pay your annual dues

And then leave....

The outcome of showing up is usually little ventured, and probably little gained. And then we move on to the next lunch, conference, meeting or webinar.

It's much more difficult to be involved in the planning.

Because involvement in the planning requires a commitment:

- Of time
- Of thought
- Of teamwork

But it's the participation in the planning stage that builds the trust. In planning, we engage with others who are working towards a common goal.... a positive outcome. And this is how trust is built. And trustworthy relationships lead to new business. These relationships take time to develop, and the trust is built in incremental steps.

It's your choice. Maintain your independence, show up and then leave. Get involved in the planning and build trust. Make the investment and the payoff may surprise you.

Barbara Brooks Kimmel

Barbara Brooks Kimmel is the Executive Director of Trust Across America-Trust Around the World whose mission is to help organizations build trust. She is also the editor of the award winning TRUST INC. book series and the Executive Editor of TRUST! Magazine. In 2012 Barbara was named "One of 25 Women Changing the World" by Good Business International.

Building a Culture of Trust

Slice n' Dice: Cutting Through Clutter to Discover How Trust is Built and Broken

Time: 1 hour

Materials needed: Flipchart, as well as pen and paper for each participant

The absence of trust in a workplace can drain your energy, derail productivity, and dramatically impact your bottom-line results. Yet identifying the root causes of diminished trust can be challenging. Below, we outline a process to help you and your team or group pinpoint the specific, measurable behaviors that detract from and break trust and the behaviors that support and build trust within your organization.

Recommended steps are as follows:

1. Draw a large *T* on a piece of flipchart paper, and label the top center "Our Workplace Behaviors." Then label the left and right columns "Breaks Trust" and "Builds Trust," respectively.

2. Ask team members to spend 10 minutes individually thinking about the specific behaviors that break trust in their relationships at work. These behaviors can be based on how people manage their work, communications, or professional conduct. They can be as unintentional as not replying promptly to a request for time-sensitive information or as overt as gossiping or sharing another's confidences. The intent of this portion of the exercise is to draw out both the minor and major ways trust is tested or broken on a daily basis through specific, identifiable behaviors.

3. Repeat this process for behaviors that build trust in the organization. Again, the behaviors can be identified in how people act, speak, or manage tasks. Examples may include giving recognition for others' contributions when it's not strictly necessary to do so, taking extra time to carefully manage expectations, or taking responsibility for mistakes made.

4. Ask each team or group member in turn to offer behaviors from their list. As each behavior is added to the appropriate column on the

flipchart, ask for a show of hands of those who'd also included them on their lists. Tally results next to each behavior on the flipchart.

5. Select the three behaviors that break trust most often (those with the highest tallies). These represent your team or group's greatest opportunities for restoring and strengthening trust.

6. Strategize ways to resolve these three trust breaking/challenging behaviors. Options could include creating regular safe forums for team members to constructively share feelings (and the impact) generated by these behaviors, and support mechanisms and reward systems for practicing desired trust building behaviors. *Important note:* the goal is for each person to take ownership of the ways he or she erodes or breaks trust, and proactively reduce those behaviors – *not* point the finger or blame others for breaking trust. Extending understanding and compassion to fellow team members is essential for the success of this process.

7. Repeat the process for trust building behaviors. Select the three behaviors that build trust most often, and strategize ways to increase the frequency of those actions to strengthen trust in your working relationships.

Drs. Dennis and Michelle Reina

Drs. Dennis and Michelle Reina are co-founders of *Reina, A Trust Building Consultancy.* Considered pioneers in the field of trust, Dennis and Michelle have been researching trust as a core asset to the sustainability of any business or organization since 1990. Their clients include American Express, Johnson & Johnson, Lincoln Financial Group, the US Army and Harvard University. Authors of the best-selling books *Trust and Betrayal in the Workplace* and *Rebuilding Trust in the Workplace,* the authors may be reached via www.ReinaTrustBuilding.com

Activate Personal Agency

Trust is built when people are trusted to contribute to something that clearly affects the customer or other stakeholder. This is different than helping the company succeed which does not foster trust.

Trust is experienced by that contribution when people come together into teams committed to the same outcomes for the customer or stakeholder. This is difference than committed to one another or a team's success

Trust is diminished when we are told what to do and how we are to do it as well as being evaluated on our performance.

What to do instead: Connect every person in the organization to a Customer Champion Team that focuses on one specific customer grouping. E.g. in Seventh Generation, there were five teams that served their major buyer groups: natural parents, deep greens, environmental sensitivities, new greens, and pet friends. Using Apple as an example, you will see graphic artists, music creators, visual art collectors, publishers, etc. Everyone in the business embraces a customer to support and become expert on.

Once a person becomes a member of a team, they track news and ideas from their customer group members lives and aspirations, create social media pages to open lines of communication, make promises to deliver new products or services and generate ideas to improve the life of their customer group. Trust is built by pursuing the same ends which awakening caring rather than competition.

Holding monthly meetings lead by rotating leaders from different functions has everyone support everyone else. They are each trained to manage the Customer Champion Teams where they collaborate on ideas, vet them for alignment with strategy, engage as venture capital panels in funding, as well as launch, maintain, and track results. The customer's success is directly tracked by the team instead of intermediate functions or third parties who report to them (although they often contract for help). This way, the experience becomes visceral and intimate. Trust happens when they struggle together for success, versus are judged by bosses.

Each member on a Customer Champion Team also works in a function role as part of a team. E.g. marketing, production. They are chartered to carry back the knowledge and actions of the Customer Team to their Functional Teams in weekly or monthly meetings. Because every team does this, functional work is infused with real life understanding of customers rather than predigested information translating into feedback. Indirect connections evoke the experience of outcomes as one of counting, not caring. Direct experience produces caring and trust.

Responsibility Is Built-In: When strategy is imbued with global imperatives for improving social and planetary health, this charter becomes embedded in the work of the teams, and it is targeted for the effects it has on customer's lives. This way 'responsibility' is an embedded 'HOW" in what the business does and not a separate function.

What is required by the organization: Clear corporate direction embodied in a well-articulated and engaged strategy. Focused buyer groups that are real people rather than market segments based on demographics. Leaders who see themselves as resources to such teams with capability built to serve them. Funds allocated to each team for projects and celebration of success. The teams produce system wide celebrations when it seems time to 'yell a success from the rooftops."

What the organization must stop: There are several practices that derail trust. Rewards and recognition that single out some of a team that produced results and insult others who may have covered for them. There is no reward and recognition because it works against the fundamentals of trusting cultures and financial success 360 Degree Feedback is avoided, which is often an inaccurate projection of a problem onto a person where it does not fit. These are other practices that distract people form serving customers and leave them attending to their own image and position and not their contribution.

Why this works: It fosters and links to fundamental elements in trust and innovation. First, there is internal locus of control, the inward experience of feeling responsible for all outcomes, good or not so good. Secondly, it connects with serving others in meaningful and real ways. They are brought together by a concrete channel to exercise the connection.

Carol Sanford

Carol Sanford, The Responsibility Expert. Educator and Advisor to Fortune 100 CEOs and New Economy businesses like DuPont, Google and Seventh Generation. CEO The Responsible Entrepreneur Institute. Author, The Responsible Business and The Responsible Entrepreneur. http://www.carolsanford.com/

How to Create Team Values that Increase Trust and Performance

When you agree on your team values, there is greater trust and you create a language to discuss how to work together most effectively.

Values are deeply held beliefs about what is right and good and evoke standards that you care deeply about. They drive your behaviors and decisions. Most often your values influence your behavior unconsciously. High performance teams are clear about their values and consciously make decisions based on them.

If your organization has published values, it is still helpful to identify the values that are specific to the needs and purpose of your team. It's okay if they are not the same, as long as they are aligned and don't conflict.

If your organization has not articulated values, it is even more important to identify your team values.

The Conversation Matters.

To be effective, values cannot be identified by the team leader and simply announced or published.

It is only through conversation that your team will get clear about what the values mean and how they can be applied to improve team effectiveness.

Be Specific.

A value like "shared responsibility" can mean different things to different people. To one person it might mean picking up the ball when someone drops it. To another person it might mean punctuality in meeting deadlines that impact others.

The best way to explain your values is to include some examples of what the value looks like in action.

For example, one of our Seapoint Center values is *collaboration*. But that's only a word. A definition could be helpful, but we still might have different ideas about what the day-to-day behaviors are. During a team discussion, we each shared our thoughts on what collaboration looks like in action. We then agreed on these four examples:

- Engage through bringing our expertise and utilizing the expertise of others.

- Seek new ideas and approaches.

- Assume responsibility to communicate in ways that can be heard and understood.

- Embrace diversity and actively seek to understand all perspectives.

During our discussion, we had some very helpful conversations about what was currently working well and what needed to change – a reminder that *the conversation matters.*

You Have to Choose.

Choose only the top 3-5 values that are most important to supporting your team's purpose. Don't create a laundry list.

Most people can only remember up to five values. If you want to keep your team values in mind on a daily basis, you need to be able to remember them.

If you are a sitcom writing team, "fun" might be on your list. If your team is the accounting department, "accuracy" might be on your list. People in the accounting department can still have fun, in fact they should, but it doesn't need to be on the list because it isn't a key driver for successfully fulfilling the mission.

Although it's tempting to try to combine values so you can get more on the list, the discipline of identifying the top values will help your team get more focused and clear about the non-negotiables.

Don't Frame and Forget Them.

Once your values are agreed upon and clearly articulated, you have a language. It makes it easier to talk about things people are doing that feel off-base. And while you don't want to have "values police," it is helpful to have regular conversations about "how are we doing?"

Most importantly, don't ignore a values breach. If a core value has been violated, address it immediately or trust will fly out the window, and your espoused values will become meaningless.

Jesse Stoner

Jesse Stoner is a business leader, consultant, and author of several books including the international bestseller *Full Steam Ahead! Unleash the Power of Vision*, which has been translated into 21 languages. Over the past 25 years Jesse has worked with hundreds of leaders using collaborative processes to engage the entire workforce in creating their desired future. Her clients range from Fortune 500's to non-profits worldwide, including Honda, Marriott, Edelman Public Relations, Skanska, and SAP to name a few. She writes an award winning leadership blog. Follow her on Twitter @JesseLynStoner and find her on Facebook.

Organizational Trust is Holistic & Proactive

Facts do not cease to exist because they are ignored.
~ Aldous Huxley

We all know someone who has suffered a health scare and subsequently chose to get healthy. A new diet, exercise program and education in stress reduction. While most times the outcome is a holistically healthier individual, the choice is only made in the face of a crisis.

Five years ago Trust Across America-Trust Around the World developed a framework for organizational trust called FACTS. It operates off the same principles as holistic health. Our theory is a simple one. Just like the human body, all it takes for organizational failure is one diseased organ.

The healthiest people I know don't wait for a crisis to get healthy. They practice it proactively. And in our research of over 2000 companies spanning 5 years, the most trustworthy companies follow the same strategy. Rather than reacting to a crisis, they build trust into their DNA. The healthy individual enjoys a longer and higher quality of life, and the trustworthy company has greater profitability and longer-term sustainability. And while most people do not practice health proactively, neither do most companies.

Why not? As a CEO told me the other evening over a glass of wine, "I like that word trust. I never considered it as a business strategy."

Don't wait for the next crisis to get healthy. Build trust into your business agenda, and practice it proactively. If you don't know how, we can help.

Barbara Brooks Kimmel

Barbara Brooks Kimmel is the Executive Director of Trust Across America-Trust Around the World whose mission is to help organizations build trust. She is also the editor of the award winning TRUST INC. book series and the Executive Editor of TRUST! Magazine. In 2012 Barbara was named "One of 25 Women Changing the World" by Good Business International.

Role Play exercise about trust "The Missed Promotion"

This exercise takes the form of a conversation between Pat and Sam (either name could be male or female). Pair up people and have each person read only his or her information sheet.

Information for PAT

Your name is Pat, and you are a Quality Group Leader in your organization.

You have been passed over for promotion to Quality Manager in favor of Ann, who has 3 years less seniority than you in the company. She also has a track record of some problems dealing with people, while your history has been excellent.

Ann is younger than you and very attractive. Your Division Manager, Sam seems to like working with Ann more than you. They seem to have a very good chemistry working together. You suspect it is their comfort level together that has caused Ann's promotion, which ignores the fact that you are much more qualified for the job.

You have asked to speak with Sam about your deep disappointment at not getting selected to be the new Quality Manager. You feel Sam cannot be trusted to act in the best interest of you or the organization, yet you do not want to burn any bridges because Ann may not last very long in her new position. Your objective is to at least get Sam to admit the favoritism as the chief reason for Ann's promotion.

Information for SAM

Your name is Sam, and you are the <u>Division Manager</u> in your organization.

Your CEO has insisted that you promote a young and very attractive engineer named Ann to the position of Quality Manager. He says it is to further the cause of diversity in the organization, but you believe he just wants to spend more time in meetings with her. The CEO has requested you not divulge his prompting of the promotion of Ann as he feels it might stir up trouble in the ranks.

You complied with your CEO and promoted Ann last week because you had no choice. In doing so, you had to pass over Pat, who would have been your first choice for the job if you had a vote. Pat is conscientious and has more knowledge of the quality functions than Ann. Pat also has not had any problems with the technicians, while Ann has had some problems due to jealousy relating to her good looks. Pat would have been a much better choice for the Quality Manager position.

You recognize Pat is upset and wants to talk it over with you. Your objective is to try to regain the lost trust between you and Pat without putting your own position with the CEO in jeopardy. Try to get Pat to focus on the future rather than this set back. Make sure Pat feels valued by the organization.

Let the two participants discuss the situation with Sam not revealing that the decision was the CEO's. Sam tries to justify something that is clearly wrong. The discussion does not go well at all.

Debrief information and questions:

Reveal the true nature of the problem to Pat.

Ask if anything Sam said made Pat feel any better or did the conversation make things worse.

Point out that the true dilemma is between Sam and the CEO, not Sam and Pat.

Explore what would have happened if Sam had revealed the truth to Pat.

Trust link discussion:

Sam is in a real bind here. If Sam reveals that the CEO made the decision, then Sam has disobeyed orders from above. Pat would immediately go to the CEO to complain, and the betrayal would be revealed.

If Sam does not reveal the true decision process, then nothing will satisfy Pat that this was anything but blatant favoritism.

The solution is to play back the tape to the prior week when the CEO was insisting Sam promote Ann but not reveal why. This is when Sam should have been willing to do the dirty deed only if the CEO would take the rap or that the CEO would provide Sam with some logic that could be acceptable to Pat.

This kind of situation is actually pretty common, but it has many different forms and disguises. The real question is whether Sam wants to continue to work for a boss who makes decisions on the basis of looks and not talent.

Bob Whipple

Bob Whipple (AKA "The Trust Ambassador") is CEO of Leadergrow Inc., an organization dedicated to the development of leaders. He has written four books on trust and leadership and has made contributions to several other trust books. He has written hundreds of articles on Trust and Leadership topics. Bob was named one of the top 15 thought leaders in Leadership Development by Leadership Excellence Magazine and has been named one of the top 100 thought leaders in Trustworthy Business by Trust Across America: Trust Around the World.

Symbol of Trust Activity

Purpose: To illustrate, discuss, and understand that trust between people is based on perceptions. Every person has a different view, concept, or idea about what trust is based on his or her unique perception.

Use: Use in a training session, staff meeting, or team meeting to discuss the role perception plays in building trust.

Activity:

1. Ask participants this question: "When you think of the word trust, what image, picture, or symbol comes to mind?"

2. Ask participants to draw their symbol of trust. (Expect common symbols like two people shaking hands, a parent holding a child's hand, wedding rings, a cross, a bank vault, a heart, etc.)

3. Have participants pick a learning partner, gather in triads, or work with their table group to share their symbol and describe why it represents trust.

4. Ask for a few volunteers to share their symbol of trust. Facilitate a large group discussion about the variation in the symbols. The key learning point is that trust is based on perceptions, and perceptions are formed by the behaviors people use. If we want to be more trustworthy, we need to act more trustworthy! When deciding to trust someone, we need to examine their behaviors and not just what they say.

Randy Conley

Randy is the Vice President of Client Services & Trust Practice Leader for The Ken Blanchard Companies. He works with clients around the globe helping them design & deliver training and consulting solutions that build trust in the workplace and oversees Blanchard's client delivery operations. He has been named a Top 100 Thought Leader in Trustworthy Business Behavior by Trust Across America. Randy holds a Masters Degree in Executive Leadership from the University of San Diego. You can follow Randy on Twitter @RandyConley where he shares thoughts on leadership and trust.

Trustworthy or Untrustworthy? How Are You Perceived by Others?

What's that expression…. "Kids say the darnedest things?" Well so do adults.

Lately, I've heard and seen some great examples of trust-busting comments and actions. They generally fall into one of these categories:

- Bad-mouthing a coworker, colleague, competitor or better yet, your boss

- Placing blame before all the facts have been gathered

- Spinning the truth

- Speaking with "big" meaningless words (psychobabble)

- Crying wolf

- Taking undeserved credit

- Fast finger pointing

- Pleading the "5th"

- Refusing to admit a mistake or apologize

- Pulling a "disappearing act" or playing the "silence" game.

How many times in the course of a day do you sound or appear untrustworthy? Learn to think before you speak, and consider the potential consequences of your actions. These are quick, easy and simple ways to build trust.

Barbara Brooks Kimmel

Barbara Brooks Kimmel is the Executive Director of Trust Across America-Trust Around the World whose mission is to help organizations build trust. She is also the editor of the award winning TRUST INC. book series and the Executive Editor of TRUST! Magazine. In 2012 Barbara was named "One of 25 Women Changing the World" by Good Business International.

Building a Leadership Credo: A Team Authenticity Exercise

Authenticity and transparency create trust. Helping your team members to articulate how and why they choose to behave as they do will go a long way in fostering understanding and building deeper trust.

This easy exercise can be done in less than 2 hours. If you have less time, you can assign the credo creation as "homework" in advance of the session.

I've used this exercise in corporate, academic, and church settings, with groups of all backgrounds and ages. It's easy to adapt to meet your trust-building goals.

How to Build a Leadership Credo

1. Set up

Set up the exercise in a way that's most meaningful to you. Speak from your heart. Perhaps share a story of your own journey toward authenticity.

Sample wording could include the following:

It's so easy to run through our days without taking time to consider how and why we lead as we do. Days become months and months become years. Pressures, grooming, and politics all can create counter-pressures to authenticity.

This exercise gives each of us a chance to pause, and consider what we truly value and why we lead as we do. The work will take place in two parts.

We will begin with time for personal reflection as you create your credo. Use this exercise to truly reflect on your core values and operating principles, even if you sometimes fall short. This should be a reflection of what you truly believe about leadership and who you strive to be.

The second will be a time of sharing with one another. We'll talk about what matters most to each of us as leaders, and how that plays out in what we do. We'll see what's similar as well as the differences amongst us.

2. Constructing the Credos

Encourage each person to build their own personal credo using a combination of words, pictures, and any other creative sparks to articulate their values, principles, desired outcomes, and challenges (can be done as a "homework" assignment).

Invite participants to be as creative as they possible. If you're doing this on-site, provide poster board or easel sheets, pictures, markers, and other art supplies. Participants with laptops may also choose to create their credo electronically.

Each credo should include the following components:

- Core leadership values (e.g. integrity, transparency)

- Operating principles (e.g. develop strong peer relationships; follow-through)

- Desired outcomes ("As a result of my leadership this year_____")

- Challenges (What sometime gets in the way of living my leadership credo is…)

3. Gallery Walk

Provide each participant with 6 dot stickers for "voting" (3 yellow and 3 blue). Have each team member walk around the room and share their credos with one another. Give them enough time and space to really listen to one another's point of view and to identify similarities and differences. When they are struck by the message or creativity of a particular credo, they can recognize their colleague with a yellow dot for depth of thinking or a blue dot for creativity. You can reward the most dots in several creative ways.

Of course for a smaller team, you can always just sit in a circle and have each person share.

4. Discussion

Debrief the themes and process with the group.

- What were the similarities?

- What were the key differences?

- What did you learn about others in the team?

- What are the common challenges that get in the way?

- What support would people like in staying true to their credos?

- How can we help one another lead with more authenticity?

5. Composite Credo & Next Steps

Next take an easel sheet and work to summarize the discussion by creating a composite credo, including values and beliefs that cut across all team members.

Identify 3 key actions the team agrees to that would support more consistency of living out this vision.

You may also find value in revisiting the credo's from time to time, as individuals or as a team. Some may chose to hang the credo in their office, or to take a digital picture as a reminder. A regular check-in is a great way to see how you're staying true to how you said you wanted to lead.

Karin Hurt

Karin Hurt, CEO of Let's Grow Leaders, helps leaders improve business results by building deeper trust and connection with their teams.   As a keynote speaker, consultant, and MBA professor, Karin shares her proven and practical approach to employee engagement based on 2 decades of cross-functional executive experience at Verizon. Karin was named as a top 100 Thought Leader in Trustworthy Business Behavior by Trust Across America. She is author of an award winning blog http:// ketsgriwkeaders.com. Her latest book is *Overcoming an Imperfect Boss: A Practical Guide to Building a Better Relationship With Your Boss*. Karin knows the stillness of a yogi, the reflective road of a marathoner and the joy of being a mom raising emerging leaders.

The Trust, Ethics & Compliance Conundrum

*The ethical person should do more than he is
required to do and less than he is allowed to do.*
– Michael Josephson

In a recent blog post I asked the question, "Where Does CSR End & Moral
Responsibility Begin?" Several folks weighed in on the role of the corporation in
society. The consensus was that genuine CSR is more than just a program. It is a
way of doing business that embraces moral responsibility.

Here is another tough question. "Where Does Compliance End & Trust and
Ethics Begin?"

Doug Cornelius over at Compliance Building used the recent NFL crisis to answer
the question above in this excellent article. The answer is rather "black and white"
yet in speaking about trust with corporate executives, I often hear this statement.
"We are not breaking any laws, therefore we are trustworthy."

What is the simplest way to differentiate compliance and trust? Compliance is
mandatory while trust is voluntary. Compliance sets minimum acceptable standards
while trust and ethics are what differentiate an organization from its competitors.

While it's true that trust can't be regulated, merely being compliant will not place
an organization at the front of the pack. The legal team cannot assist leadership in
building trust, only in staying on the "right" side of the law. An organizational trust
imperative first requires an acceptance that compliance is not enough, that trust and
ethics must be embraced as a business imperative. The rest is easy.

Barbara Brooks Kimmel

Barbara Brooks Kimmel is the Executive Director of Trust Across America-Trust
Around the World whose mission is to help organizations build trust. She is also the
editor of the award winning TRUST INC. book series and the Executive Editor of
TRUST! Magazine. In 2012 Barbara was named "One of 25 Women Changing the
World" by Good Business International.

Brief, Trust-Building Activities to Include in Weekly Management Meetings

Weekly management team meetings offer prime opportunities to create and build trust between and among all members. By applying what cognitive psychologists refer to as the primary and recency effects, people tend to recall the first and final activities of meetings, similar to how people tend to remember the first and final items on a grocery list. As such, it is important to begin and end team meetings in a way that promotes trust with far-reaching ripple effects.

Depending on how healthy vs. distressed or new vs. tenured one's team, the team leader may experience varying degrees of confidence introducing a change in format. Thus, it can be easy to either put off implementing trust-promoting activities or not do them at all.

Because change requires initiative, we therefore create the right moment rather than wait for it. Too often people don't engage in trust-building activities because their focus is fear-based and self-conscious rather than trusting and other-focused. "Trust to be trusted" is an example of what I refer to as the *boomerang effect©*, whereby what you put out there, you tend to get back in kind. It is a variation of Stephen Covey's concept of "Seek first to understand, then to be understood," in that one is more likely to receive that which he or she offers first.

So how can you use a small portion of your meeting time to build trust both with and within each individual team member while building a trust-inspired, collaborative team? Although not necessary, the one who sets the agenda for weekly management meetings is the one with the greatest opportunity to introduce activities designed to create a team culture of trust.

Create a Brief Checking-In Activity to Start the Weekly Meetings:

- Because work affects home and vice versa, suggest starting your meetings with a quick, "checking-in round," in which team members can share anything non-work related going on in their life - or pass.

- Rather than offer examples, simply go first in order to provide a model of appropriate self-disclosing. Examples can include family vacations, the angst of a teenage child learning to drive, or discovering a new hobby or sport. Someone may say, "If I'm not 100% today, I was up with a sick child much of the night." Making yourself human is a big part of authentic leadership.

- Consider bringing in a prop (like a vacation picture) as an adult version of show-and-tell, something designed to promote human interest, levity, commonality, or fun.

- Model brevity. Although it is important to keep it brief, it's also important not to be rigid.

- Allow cues from others' body language to help with moderating, pacing, and timing.

The point is to allow your team members to experience "Paul or Paula the person," not just "Paul or Paula the professional". Experiencing one another in other life roles promotes one's ability to be as much people-focused as task-focused when later working together on a team project. It is a form of trust when one shifts from the perspective of "who is right or wrong" to "what's working or not working". Trust is experienced via a healthy disintegration of ego or the need to be right.

The nature of the sharing can also offer a crude measure of one's company culture within the context of interpersonal comfort and social trust. Some teams at first may find only a few people sharing or sharing content that appears somewhat superficial in nature. Give it time, because at some point, someone is going to share with some depth. It may be the life challenge of going through an impending divorce. This happened during rounds in my company years ago.

The degree of team sharing carries its commensurate level of team trust, and team members begin reaching out to one another in a show of support, sometimes sharing similar experiences within their own life.

Offer a Meaningful "Life and Living" Reference to End the Meeting: The corporate world is more focused on wellness as a viable work activity than years past. The following ideas can fit within a minute's time while conveying familial caring or levity, thereby enhancing a sense of belongingness and trust:

- End with a quote, as most quotes impart a wisdom regarding how to enhance life and living,

- Offer meaningful information or tips such as the 4-7-8 breathing exercise to help manage stress or fall asleep more quickly at night, or

- Share a brief human-interest story, news item, or joke.

As team leader, consider inviting others to share their favorite quote, tips, and such. We can begin forging more meaningful human connections with one another through small, caring gestures as simple as the aforementioned.

When we break momentarily from "work as usual," we're acknowledging the human side of one another where humor, sensitivity, and a certain sacred spirituality reside. We are acknowledging the poet, the parent, the philosopher, and adventurer in one another among many other possibilities when we share from a diversity of resources. When we engage one another on a human level that forgets titles and job roles, we are providing the kind of psychological milieu upon which trust can grow.

It is important to bear in mind the goal of these aforementioned team activities is to create ripple effects that carry over into the daily dyadic interchanges among all team members, who then can allow the spillover of good will and trust to permeate all interpersonal relationship dynamics throughout the organization and beyond.

Holly Latty-Mann

Holly Latty-Mann, PhD, president and owner of The Leadership Trust®, uses her two doctorates in psychology to heighten and crystallize self-awareness and emotional intelligence at root-cause level. Her holistic, integrative models extend to team and organizational development processes to engender trust-based collaborative efforts, thereby expediting both the creation and delivery of her clients' innovative products and services. To contact Holly and learn more, visit www.leadershiptrust.org or write info@leadershiptrust.org.

Chapter 3

Culture Activities & Inspirations

Culture-Building Workshop

> *"I came to see, in my time at IBM, that*
> *culture isn't just one aspect of the game – it is the game."*
> Lou Gerstner, former CEO of IBM in
> *Who Says Elephants Can't Dance*

Most leaders know the importance of culture but have little first-hand experience with how to develop a healthy, trusting, high-performance culture.

Culture evolves over time. It is formed, most simply said, by "how we do things here." Culture can and should be overtly addressed by the leadership of an organization. The culture of an organization is the legacy of its leadership.

This outline of a half-day, culture-building workshop for a senior leadership team will move you well down that important road of building the healthy, trusting, high-performance culture you desire for your organization.

Using a skilled, outside facilitator with experience in culture building, call your senior leadership team to a half-day offsite workshop. Here's a draft agenda:

Culture-Building Workshop Outline
(Meeting notes are clearly recorded by the facilitator on flip chart pages, visible for all to read, and pasted to the walls of the room.)

1. Welcome, Introductions, Expectations of Attendees – 8:00-8:30

2. Culture (facilitated dialogue) – 8:30-9:15

    a. What is culture?

    b. Why is culture important?

    c. What/who determines the culture of an organization?

3. Our Culture (facilitated dialogue) – 9:15-10:00

    a. What is our culture now? (Be honest.)

    b. What is our ideal, desired culture? (Be creative.)

    c. What are the challenges to our desired culture? (Be real.)

    d. How makes a culture toxic? (Be sure to avoid.)

4. Break –10:00-10:15

5. Brainwalking1: How to Create Our Desired Culture – 10:15-11:15

    a. Place several pages of flip chart pages and colored markers in the corners of the room.

    b. Divide the group into four smaller groups.

    c. Send each group to one corner of the room to write on the flip chart pages in five minutes (in one colored marker different from the other groups' colors) as many ideas as they can generate about how to create the desired culture.

    d. Then they rotate to the next corner with their colored marker, view the ideas of the previous group, and within five minutes write new ideas, or enhance the ideas there.

    e. Then they rotate to the 3rd and 4th stations, repeating d above, engaging in brainwalking.

    f. After four rotations, the entire group reassembles to review what has been written on all the pages.

    g. The facilitator creates new summary sheets with the best ideas as voted upon by the group

6. Action plans and next steps – 11:15-11:45

    a. Using the brainwalking summary sheets from 5g, the facilitator elicits volunteers from the group to follow-up on the best ideas generated.

    b. From these volunteers, a "Culture Guiding Coalition" is formed to meet, enlist other volunteers, implement ideas, report progress, and to "keep culture on the agenda" of the organization

7. Workshop assessment and checkout – 11:45-12:00

Brainwalking, invented by innovation consultant and author Bryan Mattimore, is preferred to seated brainstorming because it gets people up and moving and has them divided into smaller groups where it is easier to express ideas.

The result of this workshop is that

- Culture is now on the visible agenda of the organization.
- The desired culture has been defined.
- Ideas to move towards that desired culture have been elicited.

- Volunteers have been found to begin the work.
- A Culture Guiding Coalition has now been formed to pursue the desired culture.

The facilitator can subsequently meet with and coach the Guiding Coalition over several months until the desired culture-change actions have been embedded into the operational DNA of the firm.

My colleague, Marla Reigel[2], and I have used this culture-building workshop approach to rave reviews.

1 See *Idea Stormers* by Bryan Mattimore, pp. 25-29, for an explanation of brainwalking.

2 Marla Riegel, www.theinspiredbusiness.com

Bob Vanourek

Bob Vanourek is the former CEO of five firms from a start-up to a billion dollar NY stock exchange turnaround. He is an organizational consultant and is one of Trust Across America's Top 100 Thought Leaders in Trustworthy Business Behavior. He is the co-author of the award-winning book *Triple Crown Leadership: Building Excellent, Ethical, and Enduring Organizations.* www.triplecrownleadership.com

The Culture is the Secret Sauce

In announcing his resignation in the New York Times, Greg Smith said that culture was vital to Goldman Sachs's success and was "the secret sauce that made this place great and allowed us to earn our clients' trust for 143 years." The scandal du jour that was once served as an appetizer has now increased the public's appetite to devour corporate reputations as the main course. This requires the Board and C-suite to be the master chefs of the secret sauce. The key ingredients are integrity and honesty. You must come to the table with these ingredients, use them to guide your decisions, and stand before the organization as a model for ethical behavior. To be successful, you must make the secret sauce seep through the organization. It must bubble down from the boardroom to the mailroom and rise back up again. It must be everywhere.

Anything less, any substitutions, simply will not do.

On how to be the example see Scott Killingsworth, *Modeling the Message.* Available at SSRN: http://ssrn.com/abstract=2161076

Ellen M. Hunt, J.D. AARP

Director, Ethics and Compliance

Ellen M. Hunt

Ellen M. Hunt joined AARP to assist the organization with establishing its Ethics & Compliance Program. Her responsibilities include building trust and helping the organization and its employees make ethical decisions. Any opinions expressed by Ms. Hunt are solely her own and are not made on behalf of AARP.

The Trust Manifesto:
Creating a Culture of Trust

Trust is the essential character-based leadership value that forms the foundation for the relationship your customers and employees have with you and your organization.

Organizational trust begins with its leaders understanding that communication is language of leadership. The quality of your leadership is magnified by the clarity of your communications; the integrity of your leadership is enriched by the trust in your character.

A leader who understands the language of leadership is a leader that followers trust, and a leader who creates a culture of shared purpose.

Character is found in the values that guide an organization's behavior, based on its beliefs and purpose. Values are attributes of the organization that create trust, inspire confidence, motivate action, and give credibility to its character.

What values guide your organizational behavior? Are they values that you personally believe in and practice? Does the organization operate in a manner that is trustworthy, transparent, and accountable? Are these values rooted in your organization's purpose?

Your organization's purpose + the values that it believes in and guide its behavior = organizational character.

Your stakeholders are looking for an organization with character it can trust. Your employees and customers want to *belong* to a culture and a community they can believe in.

Your audience is listening for a voice that speaks to their minds and appeals to their hearts. They want to believe and trust in a cause or organization that they connect with.

A culture of trust is based on your organization's character values, expressed through the organization's beliefs and behavior. A trust-driven culture will be guided by its deeply held beliefs, and behave in a manner consistent with its character.

A culture of trust is based on the character of your organization—its values in action. Creating and nurturing a culture of trust begins with communication. Communication is where change begins. Culture is where movements are born.

Transformation begins by creating a Trust Manifesto for your organization. A Trust Manifesto is a declaration of your culture: a statement, or series of statements, that declare how your organization and its leaders will engage in trustworthy behavior with its customers, employees, colleagues and the community.

These are statements of how the board, leadership and ambassadors conduct themselves: how they will *be* (as in *be*lieve and *be*have). These are declarations, not wishes. You will only use the word *be* as a declaration of being and intent.

This worksheet contains suggestions for actions and values, but it is in no way inclusive or exhaustive. This is not a strict formula, but a guideline. Include the character attributes, actions and values your organization believes in.

Note the similarities between some of the behaviors and beliefs. To *be* is to *act* in a manner consistent with your character.

1. Create a short list of your organization's character attributes.

2. Create a short list of beliefs and values that guide your organization's behavior and actions

3. Create a short list of expected outcomes: the audience or culture of trust you want to nurture.

4. Following the model below, create action- and value-oriented declarations to guide your organizational behavior.

1. Character Attribute/Behavior
Actions: We will (be)

- Accountable
- Communicate
- Honest
- Responsible
- Sustainable
- Truthful

- Authentic
- Credible
- Open
- Stewards
- Transparent

- Charitable
- Grateful
- Positive
- Strategic
- Trustworthy

2. What are our beliefs and values?
We value or believe in

- Accountability
- Communication
- Gratefulness
- Purpose
- Sustainability
- Truth

- Authenticity
- Credibility
- Integrity
- Respect
- Transparency

- Character
- Generosity
- Openness
- Responsibility
- Trust

3. Expected outcomes or recipient of trust

- Creating a culture
- Measure of trust
- Purpose
- Shareholders
- Investment
- Profit
- Stakeholders

The pattern to follow is:

We will *be*   {Character Attribute/Behavior} {to what outcome or to whom}

+ {Value} {to what outcome or to whom}

= {Culture of Trust statement}

Examples:

- We will *be* stewards of our shareholder's trust, acknowledging their investment is proof of their trust in us.
- We will *be* generous, aligning our profit with purpose as a measure of trust.
- We will *be* transparent, committed to a culture of open communication and respect.

Once you've completed your Trust Manifesto, share it intentionally within your organization, and be courageous to share it externally. When you tell your customers, community and stakeholders what to expect from you, you'll be accountable and reminded of your promise to conduct business within a culture of trust.

For an example of a manifesto based on this model, visit causemanifesto.com. Feel free to adopt the BE Trustworthy declaration from The Cause Manifesto to help you start creating a culture of trust.

Brian Sooy

Brian Sooy is the founder and design director of Aespire, a design and marketing agency that empowers mission-driven organizations to engage their audiences, lead by design, and create a culture of communication. Brian is the author of *Raise Your Voice: A Cause Manifesto*, a book that explores how purpose, character, and culture help organizations communicate mission, vision and values.

© 2014 Brian Sooy

The Core Values of Trust Across America-Trust Around the World

Are you looking for a sample statement of core values? This is ours.

Integrity: To operate with the highest levels of integrity in all that we do.

Quality: To collaborate with highly respected, ethical individuals and organizations.

To share the ideas of highly respected thought leaders who want to advance the cause of organizational trust and are not out for personal gain.

To create the most integrated, comprehensive and holistic methodology for evaluating trustworthy behavior.

Community: To build a flexible, entrepreneurial organization with a low cost structure. This is achieved by supplementing our core group of professionals with a "community" of highly specialized individuals and firms that share our values.

Objectivity: To align our organization with respected leaders and organizations that have established solid reputations of unbiased professionalism in their fields.

To measure company trustworthiness using external independent data and not allowing companies to "game the system" by completing in-house questionnaires.

To ensure that there is no quid pro quo in return for association with or participation in Trust Across America - Trust Around the World.

To fund the organization without displaying favoritism or giving the perception of an implied endorsement. As such, we will not accept any form of advertising on our website.

Credibility: To shine the spotlight on "The Most Trustworthy Companies" and help them share best practices. (We will not engage in a race to expose "offenders.")

Success: To improve organizational trustworthiness around the world, achieve growth and profitability, offer quality services, and strengthen win-win relationships with world-class thought leaders who define excellence.

Barbara Brooks Kimmel

Barbara Brooks Kimmel is the Executive Director of Trust Across America-Trust Around the World whose mission is to help organizations build trust. She is also the editor of the award winning TRUST INC. book series and the Executive Editor of TRUST! Magazine. In 2012 Barbara was named "One of 25 Women Changing the World" by Good Business International.

Does your culture and structure build trust between organizations?

We know that trust between partners is the #1 success factor for joint ventures yet only 50[1] percent of them succeed.[2] How can you ensure you're building trust with your partners? First, entrench trust-building within your organization, and extend it to external relationships.

Start with a culture and structure that channel trust-building behavior. Strategy, ethics, marketing and economics literature all show that these are critical. Of course, inter-personal relationships are important but employees come and go, taking their goodwill with them. An organization's embedded and systematic "way of doing business" build trust at a macro-level within and between organizations.

Does your culture and structure measure up?

Culture

Culture is tangible and very powerful. It's how the organization - through written and unwritten rules – understands expected ethics and behaviors. It's identifying and understanding what's important, what's accepted and celebrated, what's talked about and what untouchable. It's the official and unofficial characterization of "how we do business." It includes: values, ethics, norms, goals, communications and reputation. Reputation is included because people strive to uphold good reputations. This reinforces positive norms, which generates even more trust.

Ask yourself, your team or a group
Does your organization ...

Values

1. Live its values?

2. Have leaders who pay attention to trustworthiness? (Eg: Highlight trust-building behaviour in speeches and publications?)

3. Value long-term success over win-at-all-costs short-term *thinking?*

Ethics

3. Routinely review practices in light of ethics principles?

4. Ensure all employees understand and uphold the highest ethical standards?

Norms

5. Have leaders who demonstrate trustworthy behaviour?

6. Set high standards for excellence, competence and reliability?

7. Encourage transparency and candor?

8. Show that trustworthiness is prized internally and externally?

9. Deal harshly with trust-eroding behaviour?

10. View new relationships as opportunities to "grow the pie" rather than hoarding its share?

Goals

11. Set long-term goals and stay the course?

12. Align people towards common objectives with congruent goals?

13. Use mechanisms for joint goal-setting that consider the needs of all parties?

14. Reward teams for collaboration?

Communications

15. Show transparency through timely, complete and free-flowing information internally and externally?

16. Demonstrate a commitment to truth and accuracy?

17. Have frequent, meaningful formal and informal communications?

18. Strive for, and communicate, role clarity?

19. Continually communicate benevolent intent?

20. Help create shared meaning and build understanding? (i.e., ensure you have a common understanding of a problem, build a lexicon, etc.)

21. Seek and value feedback?

Reputation

22. Enjoy a reputation for a history of trustworthy behaviour?

23. Value its reputation and active contribution to industry associations, guilds, etc.?

24. Viewed as fair and benevolent?

Structure

Structure is a more tangible coordination of work in an organization. More than a chart that maps hierarchies and departments, structure includes formal mechanisms that determine how work is controlled, coordinated and executed. Here, we focus on: hierarchy, monitoring, ethics, planning, resourcing, contracts, human resources and communications.

In all cases, the *intent* behind the mechanism is paramount. For example, are policies in place to impose power and control or to support collaborative relationship? Whichever the case, the intent will influence the outcome. As much as possible, demonstrate benevolent intent internally and externally.

Ask yourself, your team or a group
Does your organization ...

Hierarchy

1.   Have a hierarchy that helps create role clarity and effective decision-making (as opposed to creating barriers and fiefdoms)?

Monitoring

2.   Monitor to ensure quality, accuracy and competence (as opposed to imposing rules, scrutiny and penalties)?

3.   Establish policies and procedures to create a stable environment?

Ethics (yes, again)

4.   Use mechanisms to address unethical behavior? (Eg: whistle-blower protection, Code of Ethics, Conflict of interest policy)

5.   Have an ethics officer and ethics training?

Planning

6.   Have mechanisms for joint planning (internally and externally)?

7.   Have mechanisms for joint problem-solving (internally and externally)?

Resourcing

8.   Invest in Transaction Specific Investments[3]?

9.   Allocate sufficient financial, human and technological resources for successful outcomes?

Contracts

10. Use simple contracts?

11. View contracts as a way to outline a common vision, to provide role clarity and define expectations while leaving space for innovation and autonomy?

Contracts

12. Use simple contracts?

13. View contracts as a way to outline a common vision, to provide role clarity and define expectations while leaving space for innovation and autonomy?

Human Resources

14. Ensure employees have the necessary competencies, training and certifications to demonstrate capability?

15. Ensure your representatives (i.e. boundary-spanners) are highly adept at inter-personal relationships?

16. Provide employees, especially boundary-spanners, authority and autonomy?

17. Establish performance measures that encourage appropriate behavior – especially for boundary-spanners?

18. Implement team objectives and incentives?

19. Reward trustworthy behaviour internally and externally?

20. Penalize employees who act opportunistically?

Communications

21. Use communications equipment that is compatible, available, reliable and user-friendly?

22. Empower employees to freely disclose the information needed to make the most of alliances?

The number of "yes" responses out of 45 provides a rough percentage "grade" for the strength of your trust building mechanisms. Is your culture is stronger than your structure or vice-versa? Examine "no" and "don't know" responses. Are they clustered? Individually or collectively, they present an opportunity to enhance trust in many contexts. The first step towards change is identifying the need. You've now taken that step. Next, explore potential starting points. Map out your vision; rally your champions and start building momentum one success at a time.

Dominique O'Rourke

Dominique O'Rourke researched inter-organizational trust in the context of an MA in Leadership. She is a Corporate Communications manager for a provincial government agency and part-time blogger at http://accoladecommunications. wordpress.com.

(Endnotes)

1   KPMG Global (A 22009) study by KPMG Global found: Trust between partners emerged as the according

2   Glassmeyer/McNamee Center for Digital Strategies, Tuck School of Business at Dartmouth (2006) The Thought Leadership Roundtable on Digital Strategies (www.tuck. dartmouth.edu/roundtable) according to a thought leadership round-table at the Tuck School of Business at Dartmouth University.

3. TSIs are a special investment in the success of an alliance. Internally it could be training or special equipment. With alliance partners, it includes co-location, joint-marketing, signage, training, joint systems, etc.

In Building Trust Be First, Not Last

"Don't put off till tomorrow what you can do today." I can't tell you how many times I heard that expression as a child. It's one I've passed along to my own kids.

I remember one particular night during my senior year in high school. I waited until the last minute to type a research paper (pre-computer, no "save" feature.) Before the typewriter ever had a chance to cool off, and in my hurry to meet the deadline, I took the only original typed copy and tore it into pieces. The marked-up draft sat unscathed. Suffice it to say, it was a long night.

When we rush to get things done, because we've waited until the last minute, oftentimes, the output is far from ideal. We may find that:

- Haste makes waste (the end product is subpar)
- Internal stress increases
- Something gets in the way of completing the job (we tear up the wrong paper, the computer crashes, an emergency arises)
- We make excuses
- We ask for an extension
- We don't remember to do the work at all.

In business, being last to

- finish an assignment
- to show up at a meeting
- to meet a commitment or a deadline

may be an indication of a lack of competence, credibility and consistency, considered by some to be the main attributes of trust.

It is often said to give more work to the busiest person on the team. Perhaps it's because they rarely finish last.

Barbara Brooks Kimmel

Barbara Brooks Kimmel is the Executive Director of Trust Across America-Trust Around the World whose mission is to help organizations build trust. She is also the editor of the award winning TRUST INC. book series and the Executive Editor of TRUST! Magazine. In 2012 Barbara was named "One of 25 Women Changing the World" by Good Business International.

Chapter 4

Interpersonal Activities & Inspirations

A "Walk on the Beach" for Trust

Introduction

Not all of our business relationships are perfect. In fact, too many of them are far from it. Yet merely recognizing that reality doesn't do anything for us; it doesn't make things better. The *quo* remains *status*, conflicts are buried, work-arounds are devised, and while an easy (or uneasy) peace may reign, the underlying problem remains unresolved. It doesn't go away. It becomes an opportunity missed. And it doesn't have to be that way.

The purpose of this assignment and subsequent action is to provide you with an opportunity to focus on improving one or more of your important working relationships in a way that has not occurred before. The first part of the process entails completing six key questions in advance. You will then spend some uninterrupted time with your counterpart in a setting away from the workplace, a so-called "walk on the beach", where you will describe and discuss your respective responses to the key questions. While at the outset there may naturally be a sense of apprehension, risk or discomfort in addressing things so directly, it will be apparent upon completion just how much has been accomplished merely by having had the conversation.

There are four prerequisites for a successful experience and a worthwhile outcome:

1. **A belief that a relationship has the possibility of improvement.**
   If you firmly, deeply, truly believe there really is *zero* chance of improving a particular relationship, that in effect, you are "done with it", then don't spend the time doing this. The very fact that the other person might hold out some hope for the relationship, or is willing to do this walk may help you reconsider your view. If it does not, be ready to discuss with them why you are unwilling to try.

2. **Some initial diligence on your part** in the completion of the six key questions beforehand. It will take you 30 minutes or more if you are going to do it justice.

3. **An absolute pact of confidentiality** on the part of both you and your counterpart. What is written down, what is read, and what is said should not be shared with any other colleague. At the end of your "walk", the two of you should explicitly discuss what generic phrases each or both of you will say if someone asks you how it went, what you said, or what the other person said. Your answer might be

something along the lines of: *"It went well."* Or, *"We talked about a whole bunch of stuff."* No specific content should be shared. It's just not fair to do that to yourself or to the other person.

4.   **A commitment to tell each other the truth.** In some situations, it will be your first, best opportunity to do something like this, and to build some new relationships. In other situations, this represents your last, best and only chance to make things work. Don't try to fake it just to be compliant. It is too important for you, for them, and for your organization.

The Process

1.   Respond to the key questions on the template. Fill it out by hand. Give yourself the necessary time to prepare the thoughtful responses this deserves.

2.   Fix a time and a place for you and your counterpart to meet. In person. Not electronically or while in a car or on a plane. Budget about two hours for this meeting. If all you do is swap answers and finish in an hour, you have merely gone through the motions and you won't have had a meaningful conversation. Please DON'T do this at the office, or at a place where you are likely to see colleagues. Find a place that is hopefully interesting and appealing and conducive to conversation. Some people do half over lunch, and half on a walk. Others find a quiet-enough spot in a museum, in a park or at a monument. As long as you can see each other and hear each other speak, the location is up to you.

3.   Go through the template question by question with each other in turn, one question at a time. Read your response to the other person. Explain it as necessary. Ask questions of each other. Ask for clarifications or examples as you need them. Try to hold off on challenging or disagreeing with someone until you have each gone through the six questions. You will have far greater context and perspective that way.

4.   You should each also take a blank copy of the template with you, for you to take notes on what you hear. Don't just hand a copy of your template over to your counterpart at the beginning of the conversation. Let them hear you discuss your answers and take notes.

5.   There is no expected or mandated report-out when you are finished.

No submission of action steps, no report-back to a central authority, no handing in of your notes. The only explicit requirement is that you have done your best to truly take in what your counterpart is saying, or attempting to say. That said, you may also want to consider how best to help, truly help this other person as they work with you and others. That is for the two of you to decide.

Response Template: Six Key Questions

1. The best parts of working with you are...

2. The hardest parts of working with you are...

3. Here's what I need from you that I'm not currently getting, or need more of (and here's how you could provide it)...

4. Here's what I am getting from you that I don't need, or need less of....

5. Here's what I could do for you...

6. Here's my wish for us...

Copyright 2014, Center for Leading Organizations

Rob Galford

Rob Galford (rgalford@centerforleading.com) is Managing Partner of the Center for Leading Organizations, and a Leadership Fellow in Executive Education at the Harvard Graduate School of Design. He is a member of the Board of Directors of Forrester Research (NASDAQ:FORR), where he chairs the Compensation and Nominating Committee and serves as an outside board advisor to the noted architectural firm, Shepley, Bulfinch. He is the co-author of The Trusted Advisor, The Trusted Leader, and Your Leadership Legacy, and numerous articles and blogs on leadership and governance for Harvard Business Review, Inc. Magazine, and other major publications.

Life is a Series of Small Interpersonal Transactions

Curtis C. Verschoor, CMA, a member of the IMA Committee on Ethics and one of Trust Across America's Top Thought Leaders in Trustworthy Business Behavior recently wrote a blog post called A Disturbing Thirty Days

http://www.accountingweb.com/article/disturbing-thirty-days/219658

Essentially, the post talks about the enormous worldwide corporate transgressions that occurred from mid-June to mid-July 2012 beginning with $4 billion in fraud and ethics fines levied against the pharmaceutical industry. The enormity of these global trust violations is staggering.

Life is a series of small interpersonal transactions that either build trust or lose trust. I believe that the economics of trust works as follows: every small positive deed, whether seen or unseen, adds to ones personal and professional value. In this environment, a single transgression can derail decades worth of "brand" building if trust has not been "banked".

Lately I've thought quite a bit about trust violations and what's behind them. In most cases, the root cause of the breakdown of trust is self-serving and self-interested behavior, often on the part of those in the most trusted positions in business. While all professionals, regardless of their field, can build and bank trust, sadly few choose to. Even those who work in the fields of trust and ethics don't always take the high road. And so here we are today witnessing some of the worlds largest companies paying billions of dollars in fraud and ethics fines, with no apparent end in sight.

Most of us have fallen victim to trust violations, and while the "big" cases, like those referenced in the link above, make the news, the day-to-day transgressions may not. Regardless of their size, trust violations harm interpersonal, inter-organizational and international relations.

Franklin Delano Roosevelt's second inaugural address in 1937 included the following passage. "We have always known that heedless self interest was bad morals, we now know that it is bad economics. Out of the collapse of a prosperity whose builders boasted their practicality has come the conviction that in the long run economic morality pays." Roosevelt was correct. Economic morality does pay but it seems that the business world needs a reminder.

Barbara Brooks Kimmel

Barbara Brooks Kimmel is the Executive Director of Trust Across America-Trust Around the World whose mission is to help organizations build trust. She is also the editor of the award winning TRUST INC. book series and the Executive Editor of TRUST! Magazine. In 2012 Barbara was named "One of 25 Women Changing the World" by Good Business International.

Maverick Project Role Play

This is a role-play exercise between two individuals. They first read their version of the case and then have a discussion.

You are Alan (The CEO)

Yesterday, you made an announcement that the Maverick Project is going to be defunded immediately. The project was one of three that was lagging behind expectations. You have discussed several times with Lou (the program manager) that time is running out. With the severe pressure on profitability, you can no longer justify trying to make the Maverick concept into a viable product. You doubt that it will ever work.

You recognize that Lou will not be happy about the decision, but you have given an extra six months for the team to launch the product. They keep thinking a breakthrough is at hand, but twice before these hopeful events have proven to be false alarms.

The handwriting has been on the wall for some time, and it is time to reallocate the resources to other projects. You have been a big supporter of Lou and the entire Maverick Project Team, and the cancelation decision was not a slam of them. It was just a prudent business decision that had to be made.

In making your decision and announcement, you did not expect anyone to be surprised at all. Sure they will be sad, but they should easily understand the logic. Lou has asked to discuss the announcement with you today.

You are Lou (Program Manager of the Maverick Project)

You have been working with a team on a new "Maverick" product for the company for 3 years. It has the potential to make huge profits for the organization, but it has had a couple technical difficulties that have resulted in it being more difficult to accredit than originally thought. The launch date has slipped out several months. The team has seen some really encouraging signs over the past two weeks, and last weekend a major breakthrough was made, so the team is very excited. This may be the break you have been working toward for so long.

Yesterday, out of the clear blue, Alan (the CEO) made a public announcement that the Maverick Project was being cancelled along with two other projects. You can understand the other two projects being cancelled because they were turkeys with little impact on the business, but the Maverick Product was really critical.

The CEO totally ignored the recent progress of the team and cut the legs out from under you as a leader. In the past, he has always supported the team and the work on Maverick, so this abrupt announcement is shocking.

You have asked to talk with Alan today because you are so angry that you are considering resigning from the company. At the very least, he should have had the courtesy to tell you privately before announcing the cancellation to the entire team. Now everyone is worried about being laid off, and just as things were looking like a home run was in the offing. If the program needed to be cancelled, you should have been the one to break the bad news to your team, not Alan. You are fuming about this.

Analysis and debrief material:

The issue here is one of poor communication. Each individual was making assumptions about how close to the edge the project really was. The CEO had been sending signals for quite a while that time was running out, but failed to keep current with the details.

The project manager was encouraged by recent progress and was convinced that there would be time to demonstrate the breakthrough. Both people assumed the other person knew more than they actually did. This kind of misunderstanding is common in most organizations. The cure is to not assume and to communicate information on a regular basis. Both parties were at fault in this case.

Bob Whipple

Bob Whipple (AKA "The Trust Ambassador") is CEO of Leadergrow Inc., an organization dedicated to the development of leaders. He has written four books on trust and leadership and has made contributions to several other trust books. He has written hundreds of articles on Trust and Leadership topics. Bob was named one of the top 15 thought leaders in Leadership Development by Leadership Excellence Magazine and has been named one of the top 100 thought leaders in Trustworthy Business by Trust Across America: Trust Around the World for the past five years. Contact information: bwhipple@leadergrow.com

Trust & the Rabbi's Message

Trust yourself. Create the kind of self that you will be happy to live with all your life. Make the most of yourself by fanning the tiny, inner sparks of possibility into flames of achievement.
– Golda Meir, Former Israeli Prime Minister

Occasionally I receive a note or a call from a religious leader acknowledging the importance of trust in our everyday lives. But a Rabbi's recent message struck a chord. This Rabbi presides over a large congregation of business leaders. He said he regularly visits our website and had read our first book. It had inspired him to write a sermon about the subject of trust for the High Holidays, a period of reflection and repentance. He joked about his audience being a captive one. "They have to listen." The Rabbi acknowledged that "In most relationships, trust is taken for granted. It's never discussed. But when the same occurs in business, the implications of low trust are much broader."

Holidays are times for family gatherings. They are an opportunity to discuss trust and its role in our everyday lives.

- If you have a young family, talk about family values and what they mean. Perhaps you can even make a written list and regularly refer to it at the dinner table. Update it and modify it over time.

- If your children are older, the discussion might focus on a recent trust breach from the news- the NFL or Home Depot.

- If you are spending time with adult friends, talk about the role of trust in your professional lives and how it might be improved.

Have the "trust talk." It's a great time of the year to do it. But most important, never take trust for granted.

Barbara Brooks Kimmel

Barbara Brooks Kimmel is the Executive Director of Trust Across America-Trust Around the World whose mission is to help organizations build trust. She is also the editor of the award winning TRUST INC. book series and the Executive Editor of TRUST! Magazine. In 2012 Barbara was named "One of 25 Women Changing the World" by Good Business International.

Trust Begins with You

You want trust. You need trust. You deserve trust. The good news is, trust begins with you. It begins with how you bring yourself to your relationships. This is good news because you are in control of how you show up in these interactions. The choices you make influence the level of trust in your life - both at work and at home.

That's not to say building trustworthy relationships is easy or quick. There is no shortcut to trust – no magic anecdote or quick-fix solution. Yet, through a commitment you make to practice trust building behaviors (and minimize trust breaking ones) you can build trust in your relationships on a daily basis.

Within the choices you make to build trust lives the potential for extraordinary self-awareness and renewal. Trust begins with you. When you extend trust, you become energized by the vibrancy of your relationships and the emergence of the highest, best version of yourself. You become inspired by a life lived with honesty and humbleness; with insight and wisdom; with empathy and compassion.

As you engage in the trust building exercises and find inspiration in the trust messages throughout this book, we ask you to hold in your heart and mind the truth about building trustworthy connections: *Trust Begins with You.* You earn trustworthiness when you claim ownership of *your* role in creating trusting relationships. We offer the following affirmations to energize you in this ownership of trust.

Trust Begins with You:

- *You have a fundamental right to trustworthy relationships.* Trustworthy relationships are as crucial to your mental, physical, and emotional health as clean water, nutritious food, and dependable shelter. You deserve access to trust as assuredly as you deserve access to these other cornerstones of the human experience. Trust begins with you, and your act of claiming the right to it in your life.

- *You don't need to wait on anyone else's permission to build trust.* There are many aspects of your personal and professional life for which you need to gain 'buy in' before moving forward. Trust isn't one of them. You don't need anyone else's permission - or blessing - to begin building trustworthy relationships. Trust begins with you, and your individual commitment to the trust building process.

- *You can begin increasing your trustworthiness today.* By looking at how you approach your relationships, you can begin removing the obstacles that are preventing you from trusting in others. Trust begins with you, and your willingness to increase the trust you extend to those around you.

- *You always have what you need to build trustworthy connections.*
  The energy, intuition, and creativity you need to build trusting relationships are always available to you. To access them, take care of yourself. Nurture your body, mind, and spirit. Doing so will empower you to move through the process of trust building with strength, clarity, and focus. Trust begins with you, and your belief that *you* are worth prioritizing in the interest of creating trustworthy connections.

Drs. Dennis and Michelle Reina

Drs. Dennis and Michelle Reina are co-founders of *Reina, A Trust Building Consultancy*. Considered pioneers in the field of trust, Dennis and Michelle have been researching trust as a core asset to the sustainability of any business or organization since 1990. Their clients include American Express, Johnson & Johnson, Lincoln Financial Group, the US Army and Harvard University. Authors of the best-selling books *Trust and Betrayal in the Workplace* and *Rebuilding Trust in the Workplace*, the authors may be reached via www.ReinaTrustBuilding.com

Creating Your Personal Framework for Assessing Trust

Trust is not a feeling, although it often manifest as a sense we have about a person. It is also not a function of affinity, although people to whom we are naturally drawn are often naturally easier for us to trust.

Trust is actually an assessment we make consciously or unconsciously based on our authentic answer to the following two questions:

1.   Do you care about me?

2.   Can I depend on you?

The basis for that our responses to those questions, however, is a very personal one. Some grant trust easily. They assume the answer to those questions is yes until proven otherwise. Others require that someone earn their trust believing that these questions can only be answered based on experience over time. Many fall somewhere in between willing to grant some level of trust to begin with while remaining prudent in dealings until trust is earned.

However, if you are to develop the capacity to consciously build trust with others, as well as be able to repair trust when it is broken, you must be able to distinguish the basis for which you make the assessment to trust someone or not, and to what level you will grant your trust.   The better you can become at pinpointing the source of the gap in trust in your relationships, the more effectively you will be able to design the conversations and actions that can close that gap.

Relationships are the foundation for all accomplishment. Trust is the fabric of the quality of those relationships and will make the difference in the level of results you can achieve with others. That is why trust must be more than something that happens over time in a relationship. It must be something we can and do consciously and intentionally create if we are to harness the power of the diversity of people and situations we will encounter.

This exercise is designed to support you in understanding your personal framework for making assessments about trust.

1. Choose a context for your inquiry.
Your basis for assessing trust and the level of trust required of your relationships will likely be context sensitive. For example, in a business partnership you will

likely consider different things than you would in a customer/supplier type of relationship. For the exercise below, choose one context. We recommend you repeat this exercise for at least 3 different contexts so you can begin to see the nuances of how you make assessments regarding trust.

2. In the chosen context, what is your basis for determining whether someone cares about you? Respond to the following questions and then identify the top 5-10 behaviors that clearly demonstrate someone can be trusted.

    a.   What are behaviors demonstrate to you that someone cares about you?

    b.   What behaviors demonstrate to you that someone does not care about you?

3. In the chosen context, what is your basis for determining whether someone can be depended on? Respond to the following questions and refine your responses to each to the top 3-5 that best capture what must be demonstrated for you to grant your trust.

    a.   In what dimensions/ways must they demonstrate sincere?

    b.   In what dimensions/ways must they demonstrate competence?

    c.   In what dimensions/ways must they demonstrate reliability?

4. What must you be able to say about a person in this context for you to be willing to trust them? Be as simple and specific as possible. Narrow your list to the 3-5 most important things.

5. Now choose a specific person with whom you would like to increase trust: Assess your level based on the criteria you developed above. Be as specific as possible. The point is to identify the specific source of the trust gap in your relationship.

Part I: Assessing YOUR Trust in THEM

    a.   In what specific dimensions have they gained your trust?

    b.   In what ways have they lost or perhaps not yet gained your trust?

Part II: Assessing THEIR Trust in YOU

    a.   In what specific dimensions do you believe you have gained their trust?

    b.   In what dimensions have you lost or perhaps not yet gained their trust?

6. **Develop an action plan** for increasing trust: What conversation could you initiate to begin to close the trust gap? Consider things such as:

   a. Establish a shared understanding of what is required to create mutual trust for both of you.

   b. Clear the air by communicating how you have acted in a way that might have lost their trust or what they might have done to lose yours.

   c. Make a specific request to support them in taking action to increase their trust with you or to help you to increase their trust in you?

Trust is created one action at a time. The foundation for creating a trusting relationship, however, is established one conversation at a time. By getting clear about your framework for assessing trust you will gain access to the conversations that can build the foundation for trust for the future in every relationship.

Susan Mazza

Susan Mazza works with leaders and their organizations to transform their performance from solid to exceptional as a business consultant, leadership coach and motivational speaker. CEO of Clarus-WORKS, Founder/Author of Random Acts of Leadership™, and Co-Author of The Character-Base Leader, Susan was named one of the Top 100 Thought Leaders by Trust Across America in 2013.

A Collection of Quotes on Interpersonal Trust

Trust is the glue of life. It's the most essential ingredient in effective communication. It's the foundational principle that holds all relationships. –   Stephen Covey

My belief is that communication is the best way to create strong relationships.
– Jada Pinkett Smith

If civilization is to survive, we must cultivate the science of human relationships - the ability of all peoples, of all kinds, to live together, in the same world at peace.
– Franklin D. Roosevelt

Our minds influence the key activity of the brain, which then influences everything; perception, cognition, thoughts and feelings, personal relationships; they're all a projection of you. – Deepak Chopra

Business is not just doing deals; business is having great products, doing great engineering, and providing tremendous service to customers. Finally, business is a cobweb of human relationships. – Ross Perot

Like everybody else, I've had relationships in which I was passionately in love but was completely miserable all the time and didn't trust the person I was in love with one inch.
– Salman Rushdie

*I think trust is primarily built through relationships, and it's important because it's the foundational currency that a leader has with his team or his followers. –*Tom Rath

Barbara Brooks Kimmel

Barbara Brooks Kimmel is the Executive Director of Trust Across America-Trust Around the World whose mission is to help organizations build trust. She is also the editor of the award winning TRUST INC. book series and the Executive Editor of TRUST! Magazine. In 2012 Barbara was named "One of 25 Women Changing the World" by Good Business International.

Engaging Between Generations to Build Trust

We all have varied interests. Depending on our preferences and generation, we may read different news sites, magazines, or blogs. The differences are good, as it keeps various authors and news sources in the business of writing and challenging their readers' insights. However, when reading goes unshared and remains an individual activity, value is lost.

When I read an interesting article on *Fast Company* or LinkedIn, I will likely share it in a conversation during lunch or a break. Value is gained as we exchange perspectives. Two wonderful things happen in this practice. First, we may become more firm in our views or we may add a new twist to them. Second, trust is built. Through our openness to ideas and insights, we begin to form a bond of trust. Trust does not mean we all have the same views. In fact, having everyone in a team or organization with an identical mindset will eventually erode trust since there is no challenge to our thoughts or actions. In diversity, there is accountability, too.

Today, many organizations have at least four generations working together, the first in many decades. This is a very positive element, if engaged fully. When the experience of the Silent Generation and Boomers is combined with the energy of Gen X and Millennials, powerful things can happen!

We cannot miss this opportunity to share our experiences. Older generations can share lessons learned while younger generations can share lessons of newer experiences and insights. In doing this, older generations get energized, and younger generations gain depth. A win-win in building short and long term trust.

Reading Builds Trust and Leaders Challenge

So let's combine the power of reading and four generations. To build trust on an ongoing basis, there are four steps to engage at new levels, strengthening leadership and character to achieve a greater purpose in our work and initiatives.

Step 1: Identify at least one person from a younger or older generations. If possible, select two people from two different generations. This step can (and should) be initiated by an individual from any generation. This is not just something for someone from an older generation to do. Millennials can take the first step, too. No matter who initiates, someone needs to take the first step.

Step 2: Arrange a time to discuss reading habits, likes, and dislikes. Ideally, this conversation would happen informally, over coffee or lunch. Invite one of your selected individuals to just talk about what they are reading and what they like to read. This includes news sites, books, and other articles. Use this time to understand and set the foundation for the initiative about to unfold.

Step 3: Propose the Reading Builds Trust and Leaders Challenge. The small step is to focus on articles. Every other week, each should share a link to or copy of the best article read. Once shared, carve out some time to read it. After each article is read, get together and discuss what each learned from the two different articles.

Do this for several months. What will likely unfold is greater insights on how two different generations think, analyze, and act upon the information absorbed. What also will unfold is a realization we may have more similarities in our leadership characteristics than originally thought. In other words, perceived barriers begin to erode and each learns something new in their growth as leaders and individuals. Trust forms and is strengthened.

After the small step is taken, determine the right time to take a bigger step. Have each individual share a book they have read. Take the time to read each other's book. Try to do this twice a year and don't limit yourself to just business books. Novels and biographies are a great way to understand what resonates within. Good books come in all sorts of categories and sizes so be open to share diverse types.

Setup a time to discuss what you learned from the book and what inspired you from the reading. This is an exchange so challenge each other and understand what you would change – actions or perspectives – in what you learned.

What ideally unfolds is an ongoing insight exchange and substantive conversations through the articles and books read. This activity creates a tempo between current events and deeper concepts and ideas. Trust goes wide and deep in what we exchange and learn.

Step 4: Take a step back and reflect on what each has learned. After this exchange and engagement level as been underway, take a step back and discuss what each has learned through this process. Ask how the trust level has changed. Commit to continue the conversations and exchanges. Find a way to spread this practice to other leaders within your organization.

Reading is leading, and sharing what you read is building trust. This is even truer when it comes to engaging between generations. In our workplaces, we have many ways to be good examples. When we engage proactively between generations, we show the way to build trusted partnerships to grow respectfully, solve problems innovatively, and build stronger leaders collaboratively.

Jon Mertz

Jon Mertz is vice president of marketing at Corepoint Health and writes on Millennial leadership at Thin Difference, inspiring each generation to share their experiences and raise the standard of leadership. Jon also is one of the 2014 Top 100 Thought Leaders in Trustworthy Business.

Do You Have an Accountability Plan?

Recently, a friend relayed a story about a colleague who is ALWAYS 10 minutes late for meetings. She said she "trusts" this person to always be late. We laughed about the (mis)use of the word "trust" and moved on. But what my friend is doing is forgiving her colleague for her lack of accountability by ignoring her tardiness. I'll bet nobody has ever spoken to this person about arriving on time. Accountability is a large component of trust, but one of the least discussed.

So how do you build accountability into your organization?

Be the Role Model: Leaders can't demand accountability without first modeling it. Deliver on your expectations and do what you say you will do. Then, set up the following action plan to instill its importance in your team:

- **Role identification:** Team members need to understand their roles.

- **Expectations & Goals:** Identify them in a way that the team understands and accepts.

- **Don't Be a Dictator:** Work the accountability plan together. Get the early "buy-in."

- **Discuss it:** Place the plan on the agenda for discussion, and make modifications, with the team, when needed.

- **No Excuses:** Once the accountability plan is in place, enforce it as the leader and encourage it between team members. No excuses for:

1. Missing deadlines
2. Tardiness
3. Too many mistakes
4. Low quality output
5. Showing up late to the meeting.

The outcome of an accountability plan is trust. It's a win/win!

Barbara Brooks Kimmel

Barbara Brooks Kimmel is the Executive Director of Trust Across America-Trust Around the World whose mission is to help organizations build trust. She is also the editor of the award winning TRUST INC. book series and the Executive Editor of TRUST! Magazine. In 2012 Barbara was named "One of 25 Women Changing the World" by Good Business International.

Creating the Voice of Trust

In leadership, clear and effective communication is essential. Choosing words that accurately convey your desired meaning, and being able to follow through on what you said, even when it is difficult or unpopular is all part of the package. However, the *image* of leadership is often made or broken by *how* those words and actions are delivered, and the perceived authenticity and sentiment they transmit. As the saying goes, "It's not what you say, it's how you say it," but too frequently, we don't realize that the way a message sounds to us in our heads is not the same way it sounds to others after it rolls off our tongues. Common statements can have very different implications depending on how they sound, and little changes can have big effects.

The objective of this simple exercise it to increase the awareness of, and ability to control the relationship between your vocal delivery and your message delivery, so that the listener accurately hears and understands both the content and the *intent*. Regular and frequent understanding breeds trust.

Warm-up

Look at the following comments:

1. That's an interesting point; let me think about it.

2. Do you really think you can have it done by Friday?

3. If we don't make a decision today, the decision will be made for us.

4. Nice work on the report; the client was impressed.

Have each person pick one of the comments and read it aloud two times: once with their eyebrows raised, and then with their eyebrows lowered, as if deep in thought. (Optional: pass around a voice recorder, e.g. on a smart phone, and record everyone's part.) After each person reads his or her chosen comment (or after listening to each person's recording,) discuss the following questions:

- Did the sentence sound the same or different? How?

- What mood did the speaker seem to be in each time? Why?

- How would you feel if the speaker said it to you with the first delivery? The second? Why?

- If two or more people chose the same comment to read, did their respective deliveries make a different impression on the listeners? If so, how? (E.g., maybe one person sounded more sincere or friendlier on a comment when speaking with raised eyebrows than with lowered brows, whereas that specific distinction was not perceived when another speaker said the same comment.)

- Do listeners have similar or different interpretations upon listening to the same person's spoken sentence?

As you can see, your body and your voice are directly connected. Stress due to one situation can affect you physically, such as through tension in your shoulders and face, which can subconsciously influence your communication in another situation, ultimately sending someone the wrong message.

Application

Take a moment to think of news you want to share with someone, whether positive or negative, an update, a request for participation or assistance, etc. Explicitly include the importance of this information, i.e. don't just share statistics, for example, but make sure to answer the implied question, "So what?" Consider what emotion you want to convey, *e.g.* is a changed deadline a cause for minor but virtually stress-free reprioritization, or a cause for urgent response to avoid crisis? What facial expression and body language (posture, gestures, etc.) would help reinforce this message?

Take turns – in small groups if desired – sharing your news. Tell your listeners who your intended audience would be, such as speaking to an employee during an annual review, or opening a weekly department meeting. In three to five sentences, make your point to the group, being conscious of how your facial expressions, body language and voice influence the credibility of your message.

After each presenter, the audience should give feedback:

- What mood or emotion did you infer from the presenter's delivery? (Indifference? Enthusiasm? Concern? Other?)
- How did his or her voice, facial expressions or body language reinforce this feeling?
- Did the speaker sound sincere? Credible? Why or why not?

If time permits, allow presenters to deliver the same news a second time, making adjustments to facial expressions and vocal delivery based on feedback received in order to more accurately convey the right impression about how they feel about the information.

Debrief:

As a whole group, discuss the following questions:

- What did you realize about the way people interpret your speaking style?

- What did you learn about the relationship between your body and your speech?

- What did you discover about a person's speaking style and impression of their credibility and trustworthiness?

- What steps will you take in the future to make the most credible impression on your listeners and build an image and reputation of trustworthy communication?

Laura Sicola

Laura Sicola, PhD, founder of Vocal Impact Productions, is a leadership communications coach who helps individuals and groups around the world develop their "vocal executive presence," which is the ability to "command the room, connect with the audience and close the deal," in any context. She has a PhD in educational linguistics from the University of Pennsylvania, and has spent nearly 20 years coaching, lecturing, researching and publishing on language, cognition, pronunciation, culture, the voice and learning. She is a speech coach for the TED Fellows program, and has delivered TEDx talks, workshops, presentations, training programs and keynote addresses on topics ranging from the art of persuasive speaking to intercultural business communication, for audiences across the US, and in Egypt, Japan, Spain, China and Germany. http://www.vocalimpactproductions.com

Trust & Apology Washing

Earlier this year Dov Seidman, the founder and CEO of LRN, called for a leadership Apology Cease-fire via the *NY Times Dealbook*. As Dov explained, "You need to earn back trust and change your behavior in a way that proves, without question, that you mean it." He was speaking about authentic leadership apologies, containing specific components outlined in the article. That was in February and since then Dov has been searching for examples. He reported on his findings early in September, having identified one authentic apology back in 2008. It came from a political leader.

Last week I wrote about the "apology" offered by Home Depot's CEO after the latest in a string of corporate data breaches. He must have missed Dov's apology cease-fire request in February. I suppose the CEO of General Motors and the CEO of GlaxoSmithKline did too.

The global crisis is not one of trust, but actually one of leadership. Until executives and their respective Boards or advisors learn how to build trust by incorporating it into their DNA and then placing trust on the daily docket, we will continue to hear empty apologies. Yes, culture change takes time, perhaps a year or eighteen months, and since bad behavior rarely gets punished, there is little to no incentive to alter the status quo.

The good news, industry is not destiny. There are many organizations with high trust environments. They are rewarded with increased profitability, more loyal stakeholders and long term enterprise sustainability, among other benefits. And, most important, by building trust into their DNA, they rarely find themselves having to apologize at all.

Barbara Brooks Kimmel

Barbara Brooks Kimmel is the Executive Director of Trust Across America-Trust Around the World whose mission is to help organizations build trust. She is also the editor of the award winning TRUST INC. book series and the Executive Editor of TRUST! Magazine. In 2012 Barbara was named "One of 25 Women Changing the World" by Good Business International.

Chapter 5

Interorganizational Trust Activities & Inspirations

Trust & the Blinder Effect

We must reinvent a future free of blinders so
that we can choose from real options.
– David Suzuki

Question: What role does trust play as a business imperative when senior executives and their teams are unable to remove their blinders?

Answer: No role.

On two separate occasions, I posed the following questions to two senior executives at Fortune 500 companies:

Question #1: How is trust in your organization?

1.   Answer from Executive #1: We have no trust issues

2.   Answer from Executive #2: We have no trust issues

Question #2: How do you know?

1.   Answer from Executive #1: Our revenues are exploding and we are expanding globally.

     Note: I call this the "shareholder value" answer.

2.   Answer from Executive #2: Weren't you listening during my speech? Our CSR and philanthropy program is one of the best.

     Note: I call this the "corporate window dressing" answer.

Ask almost any C-Suite executive these questions and most likely you will get one of these answers.

Now let's take a deeper dive

Executive #1 works for one of the largest health insurers in the world. Over 500 employees posted the following comments on Glassdoor.com. Overall, the employees rate the company a 3 out of 5.

•   Horrible health benefits (the company is a health insurer)

•   Huge cronyism issues

•   Tons of corporate politics and red tape

- Poor appraisal process
- High stress
- It paid the bills
- Management by fear
- High turnover rates

Executive #2 works for one of the world's largest pharmaceutical companies. Let's see what over 200 employees have to say about their work experience. Overall, the employees rate the company a 3 out of 5.

- We played cards to reduce our workday from 8 to 6 hours
- Employees not allowed to talk to each other
- Too many company meetings and policies
- No decent leadership
- No morale
- Leaders are inept
- Bureaucracy and never ending process

Do these sound like "high trust" companies to you?

The Costs of Low Trust

- Gallup's research (2013) places 13% percent of workers as engaged (87% disengaged.)
- The disengaged workforce (Gallup, August, 2013) is costing the US economy $450-550 billion a year, which is over 15% of payroll costs.
- According to *The Economist Intelligence Unit (2010)*, 84% of senior leaders say disengaged employees are considered one of the biggest threats facing their business. However, only 12% of them reported doing anything about this problem.
- According to Edelman globally, 50% of consumers trust businesses, but just 18% trust business leadership.
- And finally, in the United States, the statistics are similar, but the story is a bit worse for leadership. While 50% of U.S. consumers trust businesses, just 15% trust business leadership.

Building a trustworthy business will improve a company's profitability and organizational sustainability.

A growing body of evidence shows increasing correlation between trustworthiness and superior financial performance. Over the past decade, a series of qualitative and quantitative studies have built a strong case for senior business leaders to place building trust among ALL stakeholders (not just shareholders) high on their priority list.

According to *Fortune's* "100 Best Companies to Work For," based on Great Place to Work Employee Surveys, best companies experience as much as 50% less turnover and Great Workplaces perform more than 2X better than the general market (Source: Russell Investment Group)

Forbes and GMI Ratings have produced the "Most Trustworthy Companies" list for the past six years. They examine over 8,000 firms traded on U.S. stock exchanges using forensic accounting measures, a more limited definition of trustworthy companies than Trust Across America's FACTS Framework but still somewhat revealing. The conclusions they draw are:

"… the cost of capital of the most trustworthy companies is lower …"

"… outperform their peers over the long run …"

"… their risk of negative events is minimized …"

From Deutsche Bank:

- 85% concurrence on Greater Performance on Accounting –Based Standards ("… studies reveal these types of company's consistently outperform their rivals on accounting-based criteria.")

From Global Alliance for Banking on Values, which compared *values-based* and *sustainable* banks to their *big-bank* rivals and found:

- 7% higher Return on Equity for values-based banks (7.1% ROE compared to 6.6% for *big banks).*
- 51% higher Return On Assets for *sustainable* banks (.50% average ROA for *sustainable* banks compared to *big bank* earning 0.33%)

These studies are bolstered by analyses from dozens of other respected sources including the American Association of Individual Investors, the Dutch University of Maastricht, Erasmus University, and *Harvard Business Review.*

Do you think the two companies cited about have trust issues? How can we help them remove their blinders? How can we help them move beyond quarterly numbers and corporate window dressing?

As my friend Bob Vanourek likes to say. "Leaders must place trust on their daily docket."

Business leaders may choose to ignore the business case for trust but the evidence is mounting, not only for the business case but also the financial one. Trust works.

Barbara Brooks Kimmel

Barbara Brooks Kimmel is the Executive Director of Trust Across America-Trust Around the World whose mission is to help organizations build trust. She is also the editor of the award winning TRUST INC. book series and the Executive Editor of TRUST! Magazine. In 2012 Barbara was named "One of 25 Women Changing the World" by Good Business International.

Chapter 6

Crisis Recovery Activities & Inspirations

Ripped From The Headlines —
Building Trust in Crisis Situations

Nowhere is trust more necessary than when you are entering into battle — or a crisis. When all is at stake, you need to know that those who are fighting alongside you are sound thinkers, and good to their words. You need to trust them, and they need to trust you.

But today, crises are hardly predictable, so how do you prepare for the unknowable? How do you build your bank of trust, knowledge and goodwill that you will dip into if and when a crisis hits?

This exercise is all about ripping crisis situations straight from the headlines, and then creating an in-house simulation that can be used at almost any level in the organization, from the division level to the Execo level to the Board level.

It is a perfect exercise to use at your organization's retreat, in order to break the ice, and get to know how your colleagues think under pressure. For the best effect, it can work with a small group of 10, but it could be expanded or contracted, as circumstances dictate.

First, the leader of the exercise goes through the past year's crisis headlines and finds 5 to 10 that could actually happen in his or her company. Then he or she would also solicit ideas for probable crises from the participants in the simulation. The mere act of soliciting ideas is bound to surface more vulnerabilities and possible problems than were ever expected. That process alone can provide a valuable diagnostic.

Then, the leader will choose one -- perhaps not the most obvious crisis, but not the least believable, either. Ideally, it should be a crisis that has happened recently, but not one of the ones that everyone knows about. The crisis could be a natural disaster, a plant failure, or a customer credit card breach, and data theft. Or it could be the illness of a key employee at a critical juncture, theft, or a product failure.

The leader would create a timeline of what happened in the real crisis...along with a list of the critical decisions that were made in real time. Then, at the retreat, the leader would set the stage, and introduce the crisis, adapted just a bit for his or her organization. It is great to use video or news reports to set up the issue,

Then, after outlining the situation, each individual would react to the situation from his or her current position. The leader would unfold a bit more of the story, then check in with each participant to see what they thought was the right course of action. The leader would ask questions, delve deeply into thought process, motivation, strategy, and process. He or she would also encourage disagreement among the participants...challenging each to bring more and more clarity to the situation.

The leader should build into the timeline 10 unique points to stop for discussion -- from the beginning of the situation (is it time to call law enforcement yet? would you tell the CEO yet? what about the SEC or shareholders? Is this a material event? When do you call in the lawyers to the dénouement? Then, the leader can compare the solutions found by the simulation team to the solutions eventually chosen in the real case. What actually worked: What was overly optimistic? And what was far too pessimistic, even in a crisis.

If the group is bigger, the leader can prepare a guide, and break the group down into smaller groups of ten, asking each group to go through the exercise and then report out to the bigger group.

This exercise does require quite an adept leader. I lead sessions for corporate and nonprofit boards, as well as for C-suite and Executive Committees all the time... and the more inventive, interactive, and proficient the leader is, the more valuable participants find the exercise.

But regardless, it is important to try to recreate the chaos that ensues in a real crisis...and then see how well the team resolves it.

Insights into how well team members work under pressure always reveal themselves, and this better allows leaders to chose the colleagues they will trust in battle, and can better assure a positive outcome.

Participants usually come away from the exercise with new knowledge of themselves and their team members, and usually a renewed confidence and trust that, together, they can handle what comes.

And that is what the exercise is truly all about.

Davia Temin

Davia Temin is President and CEO of Temin and Company, a boutique management consultancy focused on international reputation, risk, and crisis management, marketing and media strategy, thought leadership, and high-level leadership and communication coaching. The firm helps to create, enhance and save reputations for a wide array of corporations and other institutions at the board, corporate, product and funding levels. Ms. Temin writes a Forbes.com column called "Reputation Matters" and is a contributor to *The Huffington Post* and *American Banker*. For more information, visit www.teminandcompany.com and follow her on Twitter @DaviaTemin.

Is It Possible to Rebuild Trust?

There are seven elements of a trust rebuilding process which are outlined below.

1. Acknowledgement: One or both parties acknowledge to the other that there is a trust problem

2. The Courage of Self-Accountability: At least one party is willing to hold themselves accountable for having contributed to the broken trust. This takes courage to make themselves vulnerable to the other, and to admit their part in the breakdown.

3. Engagement & Respect: This leads to an invitation to talk and engage out of respect for the other.

4. Congruence- It's About Each One's Truth: Everyone has their own truth about a situation. It is critical that both parties reveal their perceptions and views of what the trust breakdown is and its impact on them. It is an exchange of views, not a blame session. Having a mediator present may help the conversation. The goal is for each party to understand the other's point of view.

5. Forgiveness: Being willing to forgive each other enables reconciliation to begin. Without forgiveness there are only grudges, and the distrust will continue.

6. Having a Shared Goal: To move beyond the hurt and pain of broken trust, it is important to create a shared goal that is of value to both, and to have a plan for achieving it together.

7. Recommitment: The act of recommitment to regaining the trust of the other makes it real. Then their personal integrity is on the line. We all make mistakes and break the trust of others. The key to rebuilding trust in any relationship is the willingness of both parties to tell their truth and to respect the views and needs of others.

Dr. Edward Marshall

Dr. Edward Marshall works with senior teams and companies to build high trust collaborative leadership cultures and practices. He is author of the best-selling Building Trust at the Speed of Change, and is a 2014 Trust Across America Top 100 Thought Leader in Trustworthy Business. You can contact him at: dr. edwardmarshall@gmail.com

The Best Treatment of Any Disease Is Its Prevention

The best response to any crisis is its aversion.
– David L. Katz, MD, MPH

An article written by David L. Katz, MD, MPH, and the Director of Yale University Prevention Research Center, recently caught my attention. The title of the article is Ebola and Unscrambling Eggs. Wondering how this relates to organizational trust? Read what Dr. Katz has to say:

That's what we do, bodies and the body politic alike: wait for catastrophe, then scramble....

The best treatment of any disease is its prevention. The best response to any crisis is its aversion.

Alas, we- anybody and the body politic, alike- seem to harbor an aversion to just that approach. We are forewarned again and again, but never quite manage to be forearmed. We wait for the inevitable fall, then dash in madly to unscramble our eggs.

By all means, let's do what we always do: call in the King's horses and the King's men, at the customary high cost in dollars and human potential. And why not, while we're at it, go ahead and cross our fingers.

The global trust crisis continues simply because leaders do not practice prevention. They wait for the fall and then call in the crisis team to "rebuild" something called "trust" that never existed in the first place. Rather than being part of the organizational DNA and reinforced daily, trust is almost always taken for granted. And often, when the organizational crisis strikes, the empty trust bank account makes it impossible for the King's horses and King's men to put Humpty together again.

Barbara Brooks Kimmel

Barbara Brooks Kimmel is the Executive Director of Trust Across America-Trust Around the World whose mission is to help organizations build trust. She is also the editor of the award winning TRUST INC. book series and the Executive Editor of TRUST! Magazine. In 2012 Barbara was named "One of 25 Women Changing the World" by Good Business International.

Appendix

Where to Go for More Information on Organizational Trust

Our Other Books

Trust Inc.: Strategies for Building Your Company's Most Valuable Asset.

Trust Inc., A Guide for Boards and C-Suites

Please visit our website at
www.TrustAcrossAmerica.com
for more resources on organizational trust.

Made in the USA
San Bernardino, CA
07 August 2015